Why We Need the Pope

The Necessity and Limits of Papal Primacy

Karl-Heinz Ohlig

Translated by Dr. Robert C. Ware

ABBEY PRESS • St. Meinrad, Indiana 47577 • 1975

The present work is a translation of
Braucht die Kirche einen Papst?, published by
Matthias-Grünewald-Verlag and Patmos-Verlag in 1973.

© 1975 by, St. Meinrad Archabbey, Inc.
Library of Congress Catalog Card Number: 75-19924
ISBN: 0-87029-053-3

Printed in the U.S.A.

WHY WE NEED THE POPE

Contents

Preface

Papal primacy, as presently exercised, constitutes a block both to further development of the ecumenical movement and to reform movements within the Catholic Church. Superficially observed, however, the decisions of Vatican I in 1870 seem to render this exercise legitimate. Indeed, the dogma seems to demand it.

It is no help merely to wish for reform. What is needed is a *theological* discussion of the conceptions which have grown up around the primacy. There is no value in opposing opinion to opinion, approving papal primacy or denying it. We have to try to *understand* this phenomenon and thus find a criterion for its further development.

The prominence of Roman bishops in the Church is the result of a 2,000-year-long historical process. We can, therefore, discuss it in any substantial way only on the basis of a sound knowledge of its origin and development. We cannot dispense with a concern for history.

In at least one respect historical knowledge will have a "demythologizing" effect. It indicates very clearly that the form of the papacy defined by Vatican I, with its absolute power of primacy and magisterial "infallibility," is not founded in the New Testament. Neither is it the original constitutional form of the Church, nor even that of the Catholic Church throughout its history.

No new findings are needed to reach this conclusion. Information contained in existing Catholic literature is sufficient by itself to warrant such a conclusion. Consequently in this study I have sought by and large only to present the state of *Catholic* historical-critical research. For the most part I cite Catholic authors.

The reflections in Part Two are conclusions from the history of the development of the papal primacy sketched briefly in Part One. The reader who is short of time or not interested in all the details of this historical development might, therefore, perhaps best begin with a cursory look at the italicized passages at the beginning of each section in Part One.

The present study is an abridged version of a course given in the winter semester of 1971-72 at the University of Saarland. Excerpts have been and will be published in the periodical *Imprimatur,* beginning with Vol. 4 (1971), No. 8.

For her suggestions as to methodological and stylistic corrections, and for reading the corrected text, I wish to thank Mrs. Brigitte Blasius in Saarbrucken.

Introduction

A. The Decisions of Vatican I

In March, 1896, Ignaz von Döllinger, the most important Church historian of that time, published a series of newspaper articles on the history of the papacy in the *Augsburg Allgemeine Zeitung*. That same year Döllinger and his friends expanded these articles into a book called *The Pope and the Council,* which was published under the pseudonym "Janus." In the foreword to the first edition of his book, Döllinger expressed his fears about the decisions of the upcoming (First) Vatican Council.

> We have written under a pall of apprehension about the grave and threatening danger, first of all, to the Catholic Church and her internal situation. However, this threat assumes still greater proportions. How can it be otherwise with an organization comprising 180 million people? It takes the form of a tremendous social problem that affects church groupings and nations outside the Catholic Church. . . .
>
> We are of like mind, *first of all,* with all those who are convinced that the Catholic Church cannot stand aloof in inimical resistance to the principles of political, intellectual, and religious freedom and self-determination insofar as these principles are understood in a Christian sense and are, indeed, drawn from the spirit and letter of the Gospel. Moreover, the Catholic Church must seek to share these principles in a positive fashion and to work in a purifying and ennobling way for their realization. *Second,* we share the opinion of

1

those who consider an extensive and thorough reformation of the Church to be necessary and inevitable, however long it may be postponed.

For us, the Catholic Church is in no way identical with papalism. Thus, notwithstanding outward Church communion, internally we are profoundly divided from those whose churchly ideal is a universal kingdom ruled spiritually and, where possible, even politically by a single monarch. This is a kingdom of compulsion and oppression. . . .[1]

Döllinger clairvoyantly discerned the looming danger. The Catholic Church was about to be refashioned into a Roman apparatus that would function absolutistically. By informing the public at large about the historical facts concerning the origins of the papacy, Döllinger tried to counteract this threat. He trusted to the anti-ideological effect this information would produce. His book did have a tremendous impact, but it could not stop the course of events.

On July 18, 1870, the Constitution *Pastor aeternus* was decreed by Vatican I as the result of its Fourth Session. Two basic ideas in particular were made into dogmas in this Constitution. The first was the primacy of the Pope (Chapters 1 to 3).[2] The second was his infallibility (Chapter 4).[3]

Three statements are made concerning *papal primacy.*

1. "If anyone says that the Holy Apostle Peter has not been constituted by Christ, the Lord, as the leader of all the apostles and as the visible head of the Church Militant, or that he has received only a primacy of honor and not a primacy of true and proper jurisdiction (supreme administrative power) from our Lord Jesus Christ directly and immediately, let him be anathema."[4]

2. According to the institution of Christ, and hence by divine right, Peter has an unbroken line of successors to his universal primacy. The bishop of Rome is this successor.[5]

3. The nature of the primacy is then defined more in detail. Primacy is not only an office of supervision or administration, but the supreme power of jurisdiction over the whole Church. It pertains not only to matters of faith and morals but also to questions of discipline and the government of the Church throughout the world. The Pope does not merely possess the most essential part (*potiores partes*) but the whole fulness of this power (*plenitudo potestatis*). He has ordinary and immediate jurisdiction over the whole Church and the individuals in the Church, both the pastors and the faithful.[6]

Concerning *papal infallibility* the Constitution states that, with the help of God, the Roman Pontiff, when he speaks *ex cathedra*—that is to say, when exercising his office as Pastor and Teacher of all the faithful according to his supreme apostolic authority in defining a doctrine of faith and morals to be held by the whole Church—possesses that infallibility which the Divine Saviour desired his Church to have. Consequently, the definitions of the Roman Pontiff are "irreformable of themselves and not through the confirmation of the Church" (*ex sese, non autem ex consensu ecclesiae, irreformabiles esse*).[7]

B. The Intimate Connection between Primacy and Infallibility

It is customary in theological discussion to treat the two central objects of the Council's definition, papal primacy and infallibility, at two distinct and independent concepts. Primacy is one thing. Infallibility is something else. In this view, it is still possible to discuss primacy, perhaps even to reach ecumenical agreement about it; but there can be no discussion about the thesis of infallibility. Now, even though these two concepts are not identical with each other, and have different emphases, there is still an inner connection. The doctrine of infallibility follows as a kind of consequence from that of primacy. (Nothing is said here about the matter of substantive legitimacy.)

The Church is not a public assembly, the goals of which are mainly "political" or social. It is, rather, a social gathering of persons united by a quest for ultimate meaning, which they have "answered" in a fundamentally similar way on the basis of the man, Jesus of Nazareth. Thus the Church takes its form from this question of truth. As a result, all the offices, services, and institutions which have arisen in the Church— pastor, bishop, Pope, councils, synods, assemblies—also have an irreducible relationship to this question of truth. Her institutions are not only a matter of church administration. They also reflect the truth of the Gospel.

Before the convocation of the first ecumenical council of Nicea in 325, for example, surely no one held that its decrees were "infallible." After the council had taken place, however, it was thought to be an authority empowered to speak for the whole Church. Its decrees soon acquired "dogmatic quality."

Even Protestant Churches which reject all fulness of teaching power in their Orders still show at least a factual recognition of "doctrine." The declaration of a Synod has more importance for the public than does a statement by an individual Protestant. The opinion of a bishop is more important than a pastor's sermon, although the latter can be much "truer." One can argue theologically about this state of affairs, but it remains a public fact. Even for Protestant theology the decrees of the Council of Nicea, for example, have greater significance than the opinions of some individual theologian of that time.

Therefore, when administrative and political power in the Church becomes concentrated, as in the Roman bishop, claims to competence inevitably arise. At first these are factual claims, but they soon become theoretical as well. This competence revolves around the question of truth which is the concern of the Church. In the dogma of the infallibility of the Pope this competence is formulated in an extreme way. It corresponds to the Roman bishop's extreme fulness of political and social power, his primacy of jurisdiction.

An Ecumenical Council, as a culmination of ecclesiastical competence, used to be considered (and properly understood, in the Catholic Church still is today) a similar kind of doctrinal authority. The doctrine of the Pope's infallibility appears to be a theoretical consequence of his possession of juridical and administrative power.

We can observe this state of affairs clearly in the history of the papacy. The greater the role the Roman bishop plays in Church politics, the more pronounced becomes the conviction regarding his doctrinal competence. This intimate connection between primacy and infallibility must be kept constantly in mind in the reflections which follow. The question of the Pope's primacy *is* the question about his competence in matters of faith and morals, at least in the public sphere of Church affairs.

C. The Current Crisis

A crisis exists in the Catholic Church today concerning the primacy and the infallibility of the Pope. The crisis has a number of causes.

1. It would seem to be impossible in the social situation of today simply to accept the decisions of Vatican I. Charles Davis has commented on this fact in the international theological periodical *Concilium*: "In modern, pluralistic society papal authority must render an account of itself to the faithful; it must be prepared to explain and justify its actions and be open to criticism; it cannot expect obedience except insofar as it takes care that its commands and statements, its mode of exercising its authority, are credible. To expect otherwise, to seek a blanket unquestioning obedience, is in the modern situation to ask that its followers be irresponsible infants or other-directed robots."[8]

2. More than by any other factor, ecumenical efforts are obstructed by the primacy of the Pope and his claim to in-

fallibility. As Walter Kasper, Professor of Catholic Dogmatics in Tübingen, wrote in the Catholic Weekly *Publik* (Dec. 12, 1969): "Defined by Vatican I as the center, sign, and principle of unity, the primacy of the Pope has in fact become a source of separation between the Churches and the occasion of many psychological schisms within the Church."

3. The legitimacy of the exercise of power in general in the Christian Church is the object of a more fundamental criticism. Did not Jesus make impossible in principle every claim to might and *potestas* and every recourse to sovereignty? Should not the Christian Church, therefore, be a community of brothers freed of power relationships, in which hierarchy (= a sacred sovereignty), primacy, and authority over believers are not to be found?

4. Further criticism is directed at the concrete forms of the exercise of papal primacy: the sacrality and the feudalistic ostentation of papal and curial self-representation, the obscurity of decision-making processes, the authoritarian practices of Rome with respect to local and national Churches, and so forth.

5. An unquestioning acceptance of the decisions of Vatican I has been made wholly impossible by the methods and findings of modern biblical science and by the research of Church history. Döllinger was already convinced that the facts he put forth concerning the history of the papacy would prevent the definition of infallibility. Yet even he thought that the papacy rests on a biblical foundation, at least in essentials. "Every believing Catholic is convinced, and the authors of this book also stand by this conviction, that the primacy is founded on a higher disposition; from its very beginning the Church is established on the primacy. It is made manifest in the person of Peter by the Lord of the Church. . . ."[9] Contemporary exegesis refutes precisely this very contention.

The conclusion from all these points is evident. The problem of papal primacy is less resolved than ever within the

Catholic Church. The purpose of the present study is to define the question of primacy and infallibility more precisely. It is posed as a question of *Catholic* theology which is aware of its obligation to dogmas. Fidelity to Church tradition, however, means taking it seriously within its history. We cannot skip lightly over exegetical and historical findings in an ideological dualism of faith and reason which is not Catholic. Only this historical background enables us to attempt an interpretation of papal primacy and infallibility.

The first part of this work is historical. It sets out the state of historical research, both biblical and ecclesiastical, as briefly as possible. If we are to understand the theses presented in the second part of the book, this historical section is indispensable.

PART ONE

The Origin and History
of Papal Primacy

Chapter One

The New Testament and Papal Primacy

The office of Peter in the New Testament is a comprehensive and complex problem. It cannot be treated exhaustively within the limits assigned to this study. Nor can we give detailed interpretations of all the relevant biblical passages. From a very specific and systematic point of view we shall examine the results of biblical scholarship which pertains to these three questions: 1. May one hold the position declared by Vatican I that *Jesus* appointed Peter as the jurisdictional head of the entire Church? 2. Does the New Testament give evidence that Peter held a position of primacy in the period *after Easter?* 3. Does the New Testament provide indications of a *succession* in Peter's office?

A. Jesus and the Primacy

Jesus' commissioning Peter to a primatial role later in the Church cannot be proved. Rather, it seems likely to be historically untenable.

1. Papal primacy is a particular form of organization of the *Church.* Thus the first presupposition for the institution of papal primacy by Jesus of Nazareth would be Jesus' aspiration during His lifetime to found a permanently existing Church. Only then could He have spoken about the leadership of such a Church. However, the findings of biblical scholarship seem to refute precisely this point. It is true that the Church after Easter understood itself to be called forth by Jesus in all aspects of its existence. Already in Jesus' preach-

11

ing and in the circle of His disciples the groundwork existed
for much of what later led to the separation of his disciples
from Judaism after His death and to the formation of a
Church of Jesus Christ. Nevertheless, Jesus did not consciously aspire to found a Church.

During His life Jesus lived in anticipation of the immediate
coming of the Kingdom of God. The reality of the Kingdom
was very near for Him. Consequently, planning for a longer
period of time beyond His own death or even for all time lay
out side His mental horizon.

From all we know, it seems that Jesus was occupied with
the reform of *Israel*. He had no conception of a Church
comprising Jews and heathens. Thus the Acts of the Apostles
(Chap. 10) does not base the inclusion of the heathens on
a saying of Jesus, but on a special revelation of the Spirit.

Even the word *Church* (*ekklesia*) appears only in two places
in the Gospels (Mt. 16:18 and 18:17). But only in Mt. 16:18
—"you are Peter and on this rock I will build my Church"—
does it mean *Church* in our sense of the word. Mt. 18:17 refers to the individual church community. It is hardly plausible
that Jesus spoke of *Church* in the former sense.

There is much to be said for the conviction that the circle
of the Twelve actually goes back to Jesus' lifetime. But that
circle of intimate disciples has nothing to do with a specification of the office holders in a Church which did not yet exist.
Rather, in analogy to the twelve tribes of Israel, it documents
in a symbolic way Jesus' claim to reform all of Israel.

Therefore, while Peter may well have had a special place
within the circle of Twelve in Jesus' lifetime, this cannot mean
a special position, office, or primatial function. The New
Testament seems to be aware of this impossibility. The assertions about Peter which a later time antedated as made during the life of Jesus are formulated without exception in the
future tense.

2.   Peter seems to have enjoyed a certain prominence even

before Easter. In terms of the New Testament, no plausible explanation can be given for this special position. The historicity of the Messiah-confession at Caesarea Philippi (Mk. 8: 27 ff.) and Peter's denial (Mk. 14: 66 ff.) remains contested. Peter often does appear to have acted as the spokesman or leader of the disciples, and this function is completely understandable in terms of his own personality. But it is also possible that his position as the first "in all the lists of the Twelve" is the result "of his later authority."[2]

That Jesus appointed Peter to this role is highly improbable. It cannot be simply explained, for example, by reference to Jesus' conferring the title of Cephas (Peter, the Rock) on him. However, opinion is divided on this point.

Traditional Catholic exegesis, as well as the Protestant theologian Oscar Cullmann, for example, in his famous book about Peter,[3] holds the opinion that Jesus Himself conferred this sobriquet on Simon. But the majority of Protestant, and many newer Catholic, exegetes maintain that this name originated *after* Easter. The following data favor the latter opinion.

1. With the single, editorial exception of Lk. 22:34, Jesus addresses Peter throughout the Gospels as Simon.

2. The conferring of the name occurs in various places. In Jn. 1:42 Simon receives his new name at the moment of his calling to be a disciple. In Mk. 3:16 and Lk. 6:14 the name is conferred at the time of his election to the smaller circle of the Twelve. In Mt. 16:18 he only receives it at Caesarea Philippi—though here, perhaps, there is not really any question of conferring a name; the name seems to be presupposed.

3. That Peter was the first of the disciples called by Jesus is historically uncertain. According to Mk. 1:16 and Mt. 4:18 Peter and his brother Andrew were called to be the first disciples. Peter seems to be the first according to Lk. 5:1-11, while in Jn. 1:35-42 it is Andrew who first leads his

brother Simon to Jesus.

4. In their present form, the Gospel sayings of Jesus directed to Peter originated after Easter. It is possible that a genuine Jesus-tradition lies behind the saying about the fisher of men. But only Luke's version (Lk. 5:10) is addressed to Peter alone. In Mk. 1:17 and Mt. 4:19 it is said as well to his brother Andrew, involving a play on words based on the occupation of these disciples. The Catholic exegete, Rudolf Pesch, thinks that this passage is an "aetiological" legend used to explain the missionary activity *after* Easter.[4]

B. *The Position of Peter in the Church after Easter*

After Easter, Peter temporarily had a position of leadership in the community at Jerusalem. However, none of the features of this function could serve as the foundation of a primacy.

1. In the mother community at Jerusalem, Peter certainly played a leading role in the period after Easter. In the Acts of the Apostles (Chaps. 1-12) he even appears to be somewhat of a leader of the "universal Church." But these narratives are very stylized and, in many respects, unhistorical.

Paul, too, tells (Gal. 1: 18) how he went to Jerusalem in order to meet Cephas. Although he did so three years after his conversion, this shows that Cephas was at least an important churchman for Paul. Nevertheless, it seems that, for Paul, the special role of the Jerusalem circle and of Peter already belongs to the past.[5] Other statements of Paul's also point in this direction: the argument with Peter in Antioch (Gal. 2:11-14, 15-20), and the references to Peter in I Cor. 1:12 and 3:21 ff. According to Josef Blank, "It is clear, then, that Paul recognized Peter's authority, though in the sense of *auctoritas,* and not as *potestas.* Peter's authority was not exclusive, however, for he shared it with the other 'pillars' as *primus inter pares.* It seems, then, that Peter had very little influence in Paul's missionary field."[6]

2.   It is not certain just how long Peter remained in Jerusalem. Some exegetes say that as early as the '40s he had to relinquish the community leadership to James, the brother of the Lord. In any event, according to Rudolf Pesch, Peter remained in Jerusalem at least until the Council of Jerusalem, about 48 A.D. However, he had to share the leadership there with two other "pillars," namely, James and John.[7] At the Council itself he reemerges in a decisive position of leadership.

With respect to Peter's activity in the mission field, we know only that he is said to have preached in Samaria and that he visited Antioch. It is not certain whether he also went to Corinth and Galatia, where a Cephas-faction existed. At any rate, the transmission of the saying concerning the "fisher of men" suggests that he was active in the mission field and perhaps even a leading figure.

The New Testament is silent about Peter after Acts 15:7.[8] His further destiny is not known. Only Jn. 21:19 seems to make reference to his death. The so-called First Epistle of Peter[9] may perhaps indicate a sojourn in Rome.

3.   Peter's factual exercise of leadership cannot be contested. He appears to have been the leader or spokesman for the community at Jerusalem, at least until his "deposition" by James. Inasmuch as this community and the circle of the Twelve soon took on a "central significance in salvation history"[10] in the beginnings of the Church, Peter, too, assumed more than just a regional importance. This importance was not based on his personal office, however, but on the position Jerusalem had as the central place in the life of Jesus and as the beginning of the Church's mission. This importance also arose from the central position of the circle of the Twelve as the binding link to the figure of Jesus. Later on, James seems to have enjoyed similar importance.

4.   Neither the nature of Peter's function nor its connection to his person was such that he continued to exercise it after

leaving Jerusalem. After this time, the New Testament authors say nothing more about Peter.

5. Again and again an appeal is made to Peter as having been the first witness to the resurrection (Lk. 24:34; I Cor. 15:5) in order to establish his modest leadership role in the primitive community. Leaving aside completely the difficult question of how we are to understand the resurrection, this seems highly improbable.

First of all, mention of Peter as the first witness could well be a repercussion from his factual leadership role. Much the same must be said about the projection of sayings about Peter back into the lifetime of Jesus (cf. #6 below). Many exegetes maintain that two lists of witnesses to the resurrection have been combined in I Cor. 15:5-7. One of them was a list headed by Peter (15:5); the other named James as the first witness (15:7). Conceivably this combination is the deposit of two community traditions, namely, that arising under Peter's leadership and that under James'. In this case, the fact that Peter is listed first among the witnesses to the resurrection reflects the actual situation in the community. In any event, nowhere in the New Testament is this first place among the witnesses used as the foundation for Peter's office.[11] Although it otherwise tends to reinforce Peter's role, not even the Acts of the Apostles emphasizes this aspect.

6. The New Testament places a number of statements in the mouth of Jesus about a special role for Peter. These sayings appear to originate at levels of the tradition in which Peter's actual importance *after* Easter is at issue. It is not the other way around, not as if these sayings of Jesus were the actual basis for Peter's role.

With respect to Lk. 22:32 and Jn. 21:15-19, this much is certain. Lk. 22:32: "I have prayed for you, Simon, that your faith may not fail, and once you have recovered, you in your turn must strengthen your brothers." Perhaps these words reflect the effort made after Easter to certify Peter's leadership role in the light of his failure during the Passion. Be this as it may, no more is really said about Peter here than is said about Paul in the Acts of the Apostles (18:23). In Rom. 1:11 Paul makes a similar claim about himself. The same probably holds true for every missionary of that time (Cf. I Thess. 3:2). In the Epistle of James (5:7.8) all of the brethren are exhorted: "Do not lose heart."[12]

Jn. 21, 15-19: To the triple question as to whether Simon loves Jesus, three times it is said: "Feed my sheep (lambs)." Peter is the shepherd of Jesus' sheep. This injunction appears to refer to nothing more than the actual leadership of the community at Jerusalem. No more is expressed than what can be said of every person in a position of responsibility in a community (cf. Eph. 4:11; I Pt. 5:2; Acts 20:28). Inasmuch as the conception of Church in the Fourth Gospel shows no traces of hierarchical structure, this statement cannot refer to some special *fulness* of office. In addition, the Gospel of John elsewhere clearly gives preference to the shadowy figure of the "beloved disciple."

7.   Only *Mt. 16:17-19* presents difficulties for interpretation. "You are Peter and on this rock I will build my Church...." (16:18). This text follows Peter's confession of faith at Caesarea Philippi: "You are the Christ, the Son of the living God" (16:16). Thus it can refer especially to the constitutive significance for the Church of Peter's confession. The fact that a few verses later Peter is called "Satan" (16:23) because he was thinking in such "human" terms lends support to this interpretation.

Nevertheless, these words are still addressed to Peter. The words used (rock, Church, gates of hell, keys of the kingdom of heaven, power to bind and to loose) are such weighty ones that they cannot simply be considered without further ado to result from Peter's modest role in Jerusalem. Contemporary exegesis suggests four possible interpretations of these words. I shall summarize them briefly.

A *first* position grants at least a historical core for these sayings. Jesus' conferring a name on Peter (?), the perplexity as to how words of such importance could have originated at a later time, and reference to the underlying Aramaic form of these *logia* are cited in support of this position.

According to a *second* hypothesis, these verses could "only have originated or held sway at the time and place where Peter was working and where his role was described in these terms.[13] Two facts are cited in support of this position. There is the Aramaic form of the words; Aramaic was also the language of the Jerusalem community. Further, there is the fact, generally conceded today, that these verses constitute an original unity in all details. Thus it is very difficult to distinguish between an historical core and later elaboration. But the question still remains whether or not these *logia* reach far beyond Peter's position at Jerusalem.

Günter Bornkamm proposes a *third* position[14] which Rudolf Pesch has discussed further.[15] The logion of Mt. 16:17-19 did not originate in the primitive community at Jerusalem but at the beginnings of the *universal Church*. It reflects the conflict between Jewish and gentile Christianity as exemplified by the argument at Antioch between Peter and Paul. The *logia* concerning Peter arose in the Syrian Church at a period which must be called *late* with respect to the dating of the other two theses mentioned above.[16] These sayings represent inroads of Jewish Christian thought into the conceptions of gentile Christianity. For Jewish Christians, Peter represents a guardian of unity and the *true* interpretation of the Gospel throughout this conflict. In order to bind the Church of his own time to the true Gospel, Matthew incorporated *logia* from this layer of the tradition.

Bornkamm's interpretation is indeed a plausible explanation of the origin of the text. If it is correct, then of course Mt. 16:17-19 does not express Peter's rights of *office*. Two chapters later, the whole *community*, all the disciples, are promised the power of binding and loosing with the same words in Mt. 18:18. The consensus of exegetes is that this passage is a more recent one than the promise to Peter. That means that Mt. 16:17-19, in the opinion of its author, did not intend to describe a personal office of Peter. Peter's function to watch over the correct interpretation of the Gospel is now passed on to the whole community.

A *fourth* hypothesis dates Mt. 16:17-19 even later. Josef Blank[17] says that "what we have here is a relatively late formation that received its final approval in the Gospel of Matthew. As in Bornkamm's view, the presupposition for Matthew's composition here is a clearly formulated Judaeo-Christian Petrine typology. According to this typology, Peter was looked upon as "the one who received, witnessed to, and guaranteed the original tradition of Jesus." These communities already possessed a "fulness of apostolic power," and Peter represented its *type*. In a narrative section parallel to the parable about the "house built on rock" (Mt. 7:24-27), Matthew then clarified these ideas by making use of the already existing name of Peter.

In this way, the saying about the Rock "does not refer to the *giving* of a name, but to the *interpretation* of a name." On the basis of Petrine typology the name serves to illustrate the *foundation* of faith. "As a witness to right faith in Jesus the Messiah, he is made the foundation rock of the Church of Jesus." But precisely in this case, the *logion* about the Rock does not describe some special office of Peter. "In Matthew, then, the Church's power can all be seen as belonging to the 'Petrine office' . . . totally at the service of the teaching handed down by Jesus . . Its purpose is the continuing return to the one Lord and Teacher, Jesus Christ." Finally, "the logic of the symbolism allows of no extension of this particular function" of foundation rock. "To infer from this passage that Peter had a 'succession' would be to stretch the interpretation beyond the literal sense of the symbolism."

On the other hand, Blank says, the *power to bind and loose* can be handed down. According to Matthew it was handed down to the entire community (Mt. 18:18).

8. Further more, the New Testament contains a whole series of statements which militate against any exclusive stylizing of the figure and role of Peter: [18]

—the tradition of Peter's denial of Jesus (Mk. 14:66 ff.);

—Peter's resistance to Jesus' Passion (Mk. 8:31-33);

—Peter's pusillanimity (Mt. 14:31);

—the handing down to the community of the power to bind and loose (Mt. 18:18);

—the relativizing of Peter's Rock function in Mt. 16:21-23;

—the presence of the sons of Zebedee in the narration of the transfiguration (Mk. 9:2-13 par);

—the application to Andrew of the fisher-of-men *logion* (cf. above A. 4);

—the precedence of the beloved disciple in the Gospel of John (cf. B. 6);

—the critical remarks of Paul (cf. Gal. 2:11-16).

C. The Problem of Succession in the Petrine Office

If Peter's primacy cannot be derived even in an incipient manner (in nuce) from the New Testament, then there certainly can be no question of personal succession to the Petrine office.

1. A specific primatial *office* cannot be demonstrated. Neither can we speak of *succession* in office. We must disregard here the matter of Peter's typological significance for Christian discipleship as such.[19]

2. Matthew excludes personal succession in any case (cf. above B. 7).

3. A certain centrality of the Jerusalem community and of its leader is uncontested (cf. B. 3). Yet precisely this kind of centrality prohibits "succession." *Only* Jerusalem and the circle of the Twelve are connected with the *life of Jesus.*

At the beginning, the Christian mission went out from Jerusalem alone. *In this sense,* no other community can assume the heritage of Jerusalem; no other group, the heritage of the Twelve; no other Christian, the succession of Peter.

4. Since the New Testament remains silent about Peter from the time he left Jerusalem, it is certainly impossible to make an argument for succession from a possible sojourn in Rome.

D. Conclusion

Even though a positive appeal to the New Testament is impossible in the case of primacy, this does not mean that an office of unity in the Church contradicts Scripture. Whatever grounds may have motivated its origin, nothing in the New Testament contradicts an office of unity as long as it is exercised within the substantial and formal limitations imposed upon His disciples by Jesus.

Chapter Two

The Importance of Rome
before Constantine

The period[1] covered in this chapter embraces about two hundred years, from about the year 100 to the beginning of the fourth century. It is difficult to put order into the many fragmentary documents from this period: detailed study is not possible here. Rather, we shall examine the current state of knowledge about this period with three questions in mind.
1. How important was the Roman community and its bishop at that time?
2. Are the traditions trustworthy which tell of Peter's stay in Rome?
3. When did Rome begin to appeal to the Petrine succession in order to establish its special role in the Church? The answers to these questions are important if we are to evaluate critically Vatican I's statement about the unbroken continuity in the succession of the primacy.

A. The Actual Importance of Rome

In the period before Constantine, the community at Rome and its bishops had already achieved a certain recognition within the Church. Even in its beginnings, however, the importance of this recognition had nothing to do with any theological function of primacy. The prestige of the Roman Church resulted from Rome's political importance, and also from its apostolic character. Moreover, for nearly the first hundred years of its Christian history Rome did not even have a bishop. It was directed by a collegium.
1. As the capital of the Roman Empire, Rome was the

middle point of the world at that time. Moreover, in spite of its size the Roman State was essentially a *city-state* ruled from Rome. Thus Rome had an incomparably greater importance than does a contemporary capital. "Pagan poets celebrated the city of Rome as head of the world because it was the political, economic, and even spiritual center of the Roman Empire. This metropolis determined the standard of life in even the farthest flung provinces. Here the early Christian mission sought to gain a foothold. . ."[2]

Obviously, as a result of this situation, the Christian community at Rome gained in importance in the Church, specially after destruction of Jerusalem in the year 70 and the end of the prestigious Christian mother community there. The community at Rome became the center of information for much of what was going on in other communities throughout the empire.

2.   Therefore, it is hardly surprising that in the year 96/97 the community at Rome intervened in controversies going on in the community at Corinth. In the so-called *First Letter of Clement,* the factions in Corinth were admonished to preserve unity. Still, the initiative here does *not* express any particular *ecclesiastical* function of Rome. J. McCue remarks that "the responsibility evidenced here does not go beyond what one would expect given the size and prominence of Rome."[3]

3.   It is interesting to note that the *First Letter of Clement* is *not* written by a Roman *bishop,* but by a community whose leadership is clearly a *presbyterial* college of elders. If, in fact, the *First Epistle of Peter,* as much evidence suggests,[4] concerns the community at Rome, then it too confirms this collegiate leadership. "The words 'I (Peter) exhort the elders among you, as a fellow elder' (I Pt. 5:1) assume that an office of elders or presbyters existed in Rome at the end of the first century."[5]

The forms of church organization in the early Church were

very different in different regions. The concentration of community leadership in the hands of a single person, the so-called *monarchical episcopacy,* only began to prevail throughout the Church gradually in the course of the second century. We do not know for sure *when* the transition to a monarchical episcopacy took place in Rome. Although *Ignatius* (Bishop of Antioch, d. 117) placed great importance on setting up the episcopacy, his *Letter to the Romans* makes no mention of a bishop. On the other hand, Irenaeus of Lyon already about 180 presupposes that the monarchical episcopacy in Rome is an old tradition. Thus the transition must already have taken place shortly after Ignatius, perhaps around 130. But up until that time Rome had no bishop at all. There was no one to succeed Peter in his personal primacy. But only a single bishop could have inherited Peter's personal primacy!

4. While saying nothing about a bishop there, *Ignatius of Antioch,* too, holds the Roman community in high esteem. In his *Letter to the Romans* he remarks that it "presides over the Roman region" and even calls it the "chairman of love." The first expression reflects the transregional importance beginning to crystallize at that time in a number of central communities. In this letter also (9:1) Ignatius speaks in the same vein about the community of Antioch in Syria.

The second expression has frequently been translated almost juridically as "president of the covenant of love" (=Church). This is then understood as a reference to the primatial role. Actually this text implies nothing more than a high esteem for Rome. "Further-reaching consequences, for example, in the sense of a universal primacy, are not drawn here. Neither can one project them backwards from a later stage in Church history."[6] It is usually overlooked that the designation of Rome in this passage occurs in the context of nine other decorative adjectives for the community addressed. Thus it seems to be mainly a matter of the polite usage through which one party seeks the favor of the addressee by making a few complimentary remarks at the beginning of the letter.

5. Because of Rome's central political position it is hardly surprising that some "heretics"—especially the advocates of gnosticism—sought to spread their ideas in and about Rome. This very natural attraction of the capital city might be compared to the current importance of Paris for art and literature. Thus it goes far beyond the modest facts of the case to contend that the "heretics" sought the approbation of the Roman bishop and to use this as an argument for the primacy.

6. Toward the end of the second century, *Irenaeus,* a native of the Near East and the Bishop of Lyon, strongly asserted the position of Rome. In traditional theology he is looked upon as an early witness to the idea of primacy. Even Vatican I cited a statement of his (see below) as plausible to the doctrine of the primacy.

Irenaeus was involved in an intense literary polemic with protagonists of "heretical" tendencies. The Latin translation of the Greek original of his major work is called *Adversus Haereses*: *Against the heresies*. The persons he opposes have appealed to secret apostolic traditions and writings in order to support their ideas. Irenaeus argues against this practice: traditions and writings are only relevant when they are publicly received in the Church. Christianity is not a matter of esoteric knowledge. It is found where true apostolic doctrine is transmitted. But this is not so for the heretics; they do not stand in the apostolic succession. In the universal Church, however, there exist a multitude of communities founded by Apostles. Through an uninterrupted succession of bishops they have transmitted the apostolic doctrine since their founding.

There churches, says Irenaeus, can be held up to the heretics as a refutation of their claims. Actually one should have to enumerate *all* the apostolic churches. "We have to enumerate those made bishops by the Apostles in these churches and their successors up to our own times."[7] "But since it would be very lengthy ... to enumerate the lists of succession of *all* the churches," Irenaeus limits himself to the list of bishops in the community which is "the greatest and oldest church known to all, founded by the glorious Apostles Peter and Paul ... which has its tradition from the Apostles." Then follows the sentence cited by Vatican I: "For with such a church (*ad hanc enim ecclesiam*), on account of its greater authority every church must agree, that is to say, all the faithful everywhere, for in this church the tradition which is from the apostles has always been preserved."[8] The text is obscure and it seems clear that the Latin translation of the original is not completely exact.

The passage used to be translated, "with *this* (namely, the Roman) church ... all other churches must agree. Then the idea of primacy would be very clearly expressed indeed. It is more and more evident today, however, that Irenaeus' whole train of thought is different: "More recent studies have tended to interpret his ecclesiology as multicentered."[9] He wants to say that the example of the apostolic churches refutes the heretics. There are many such apostolic churches, but it would be too long to enumerate them all. Consequently Irenaeus chooses *one* of the apostolic churches, Rome, the one which has even been founded by *two* Apostles and thus enjoys a special repute. Besides, it is the only church in the West considered to be apostolic from antiquity.

With *such* a one, that is to say, an apostolic church, everyone must be in accord. This statement does not mean the Roman primacy, but the validity of the apostolicity and succession of the Church. Rome is an *example,* a particularly convincing example, of apostolicity, in the opinion of Irenaeus. The Catholic Church historian, Karl Baus, concurs too: "The famous text of Irenaeus must be abandoned as one of the proofs of early Christian awareness of the primacy."[10]

7. The North African theologian *Tertullian* (d. after 220) uses a similar kind of argument. In a passionate treatise against heretics he demands that "they should indicate the origins of their churches and the succession of their bishops, proceeding in a series from the beginning so that the first bishop has as predecessor one of the Apostles or apostolic men (i.e., disciples of the Apostles). For this is the way the apostolic churches trace their origin. The community of Smyrna, for example, relates that its (first bishop) Polycarp was appointed by John, or the community in Rome that (bishop) Clement was ordained by Peter."[11] Smyrna and Rome alike serve as examples of apostolic origin.

Tertullian writes in the same work: "If you live in Greece you have Corinth (as an apostolic church). If you're from near Macedonia, you can look to the Philippians. If you turn to Asia, you have Ephesus. But if you include Italy, you have Rome, which represents authority *for us too* (in North Africa)."[12] Here it is completely clear that Tertullian's Church has many centers, *all apostolic* churches, and that Rome is *the* apostolic church to which Christians in the West can lay claim.

8. The so-called "Paschal Controversy" toward the end of the second century is considered in traditional Catholic literature to be proof that Rome's bishop at that time made primatial claims. Of the two opposing parties in this controversy, the one faction, especially the communities in Syria and Asia Minor, celebrated Easter always on the day of the Jewish Passover feast, the fourteenth of Nisan, irrespective of whether this day fell on a Sunday or not. The majority of churches, however, including Rome, celebrated Easter on the Sunday following 14 Nisan. After prolonged dispute, Bishop Victor in Rome decided to excommunicate the first group. According to an account by the first Church historian, Eusebius, in the fourth century,[13] this excommunication applied to the churches of Asia Minor. Such an action could perhaps

be an indication of a remarkable claim on the part of Rome.

However, it should be remarked, first of all, that there is evidence that such mutual excommunications occurred between other churches as well. Consequently they do not necessarily express some higher title. Secondly, McCue proposes sound arguments for the thesis that this excommunication did *not* affect the churches of Asia Minor, but the opposition faction *within the Roman community.* This would mean that Eusebius had recorded false information. Consequently this action was a completely normal measure of episcopal discipline, "an intra-diocesan affair."[14] Whatever the case may be, the Paschal Controversy does not constitute an *historically certain* proof of a title to primacy.

9. Around the middle of the third century, two Spanish bishops appealed to Rome in order to obtain their rehabilitation. At about the same time, Bishop *Cyprian* of Carthage demanded that his Roman colleague *Stephan* depose the Bishop of Arles. Rome's position of precedence within the Western portion of the Church is beginning to come to the fore here. From all that we have seen thus far, we can conclude that this position rested on the apostolic foundation of this church by Peter *and Paul.* Thus, it is not found on a succession in "Petrine primacy."

B. *The Roman Tradition concerning Peter*

The current state of information provides a series of facts which favor a Roman sojourn of Peter, but it is not possible to attain historical certainty. Perhaps Peter suffered martyrdom in Rome, but this is even less certain.

1. There are two passages in the New Testament which indicate where Peter may have gone after leaving Jerusalem. In the Acts of the Apostles it is said: Peter went "to another place" (Acts 12:17). In traditional literature concerning the primacy, this "other place" is interpreted to be Rome, but no attempt is made to explain why Luke does not say so

more explicitly if he knew anything more definite. Oscar Cullmann says in his book about Peter: "In reality that 'other place' can be identified with any city in the Roman Empire."[15]

The First Epistle of Peter, so-called because it sustains the fiction of having been written by Peter, probably originated toward the end of the first century. (Both Epistles of Peter could not have been composed by Peter.) In the so-called First Epistle of Peter we find the following greeting: "Your sister in *Babylon,* who is with you among the chosen, sends you greetings; so does my son, Mark" (I Pt. 5:13). Since the second century (Papias of Hierapolis[16]), the place named *Babylon* is interpreted as a symbolic circumlocution for Rome. It is impossible to reach any definitive conclusions here. Cullmann will not even exclude the possibility that the real Babylon could be meant. Nonetheless, he considers it more probable that this reference suggests that the anonymous author of the Epistle knew something about a sojourn of Peter in Rome. "For the author of the First Epistle of Peter, Babylon may be related to the conception of 'exile' within the theological tradition he represents. In I Pt. 2:11 (cf. 1:1) he refers to his readers as 'visitors and pilgrims.' At the same time, [Babylon] is the epitome of corruption in a world metropolis caught up in the throes of power . . . Thus, in the author's time no other place save Rome could have been envisaged to which the metaphorical significance of old Babylon applied."[17]

2. Although there is no certainty, the evidence from the early part of the second century favors a sojourn by Peter in Rome. The *First Epistle of Clement* (cf. above A. 2) exhorts the community in Corinth to preserve unity with the words: "Let us keep before our eyes the example of the good Apostles: Peter, who because of unjust envy suffered tribulations not once or twice but many times, and thus became a witness and passed on to the place of glory which was his due, and Paul . . ."[18] In addition to other examples from antiq-

uity and from the Old Testament, Peter and Paul serve as models for the way Christians are to conduct themselves in the face of strife. Nothing more is stated here. The authors of the Epistle may have chosen Peter and Paul because they played a special role in Roman tradition. But the Roman intervention at Corinth is *not* at all based on an appeal to the two Apostles.

Ignatius of Antioch writes to the community in Rome: "I do not command you, as Peter and Paul did" (4:3). This sentence seems to presuppose the knowledge of a special relationship between Rome and the two Apostles which according to P. Stockmeier, "can best be explained by Peter's stay in Rome."[19] Additional accounts of Peter's sojourn in Rome [can be found], for example, in the *Ascension of Isaiah* (4:2 ff), fragment of the *Apocalypse of Peter,* and a reference by Bishop Dionysius of Corinth (in Eusebius, *Church History* 2,25,8),"[20] but these scraps of information do not establish certitude. Still they do give witness to a tradition concerning Peter.

3.   It is not until the end of the second century that we can demonstrate with any certainty the conviction about Peter's stay in Rome. *Irenaeus* accepted as fact the activity of Peter and Paul in Rome, stating that the community in Rome was founded by them.[21] A Roman presbyter named *Gaius* writes that he could even point out the site of the Apostles' graves in Rome.[22] *Tertullian* presupposes that Peter and Paul were martyred in Rome. From this relatively late time on there is a sound layer of tradition supporting the conviction concerning Peter's leadership of the Roman community and the fact of his martyrdom there.

4.   Excavations were made beneath the Basilica of St. Peter from 1940-49 and from 1953-57, and are continuing again at the present time. However, they have not yet produced any findings that can resolve the question of a Roman sojourn of Peter. It was discovered that the Basilica of St. Peter is

constructed on the site of the earlier, fourth-century Constantinian basilica. It stands now on what once was a steep terrain which had to be filled up and leveled by massive earth excavations at the time of the construction of the first basilica. Apparently so much trouble was gone to because, according to a belief at that time, the tomb of Peter is supposedly located at the site of the present apse of the basilica.

Beneath the basilica a large cemetery was discovered which contains many heathen mausolea dating from the period between 130 and 200. Only *one* mausoleum bears any Christian ornamentation. Immediately beneath the *confessio* of the present church a small cemetery was discovered which is bounded on the west by a wall built about the year 160. In all probability, the builders of the Constantinian basilica thought that this graveyard contained the site of Peter's grave. Hence they constructed their church on a terrain on which it was technically very difficult to build and which was further restricted by burial laws. In this small graveyard there is a niche about 60 cm. (24 inches) square covered by a stone slab; other graves are situated around it. In this niche the excavators discovered "a little heap of bones from the skeleton of an elderly man."[23]

In the first wave of enthusiasm it was thought that Peter's grave had been found. But the following evidence argues against this conclusion.

a. There is no proof at all that this was even a Christian graveyard. One of the graves grouped around the niche is for *certain* a heathen one; it contains a libation vessel such as was used for heathen offerings of drink.

b. The niche claimed to be the grave of Peter has the dimensions of a child's grave. Karl Baus makes the concluding judgment: "These difficulties taken together ... make it impossible for the present to agree with the opinion that the excavations have with certainty brought to light the tomb of Peter or its original site."[24]

5. *Graffiti* containing invocations to Peter dating from the middle of the third century have been found as well on the Via Appia in Rome. However, these graffiti are only further evidence of the tradition concerning Peter, which was already late by that time.

6. Karl Baus thinks that the most important indication of the historical reliability of the Roman tradition concerning Peter is the fact that no other community made a comparable claim for itself. "This almost amazing lack of any rival tradition is without doubt to be regarded as a deciding factor in the critical examination of the Roman tradition."[25] Nevertheless, we must at least put a question mark after the cogency of this negative argument. Other cities as well possessed unrivaled traditions concerning Apostles, without its being possible to conclude from this fact to the reliability of such traditions.

C. Rome's Theological Claim to Peter

For our purposes here we can disregard the citations of Ignatius, Irenaeus and others which were formerly and wrongly thought to be assertions of primacy. We still have to examine the following questions: 1. Were the New Testament texts concerning Peter understood in the early Church in the sense of an ecclesiastical primacy? 2. Did Rome make appeal to these texts in support of its own special position as we have described it above?

A theological motivation for Rome's special position in the Church by reference to the New Testament texts concerning Peter cannot be proved with certainty in the time before Constantine, although such ideas can perhaps be found in the Roman bishop Stephan II.

1. Reference to Peter *and Paul* having founded the community in Rome served to accentuate the *apostolic* character of this church. It did not seek to justify a claim to primacy. The very mention also of *Paul* indicates that these references

appeal to the double apostolicity of the Roman community.
As a (twofold) apostolic church Rome enjoyed a high regard,
particularly in the Western portion of the Church where no
other community could lay uncontested claim to such prestige.
2. In the ancient Church, the New Testament texts concerning Peter, even Mt. 16:18, were understood only very
rarely and quite late in the sense of an official juridical primacy of Peter. "You are Peter, and upon this rock I will build
my Church..." (Mt. 16:18): only a juridical interpretation
of this text in particular could make possible a later appeal
to it by Rome in the sense of Peter's having been appointed
to a function of leadership in the Church.

In the *Eastern Greek* Church, Mt. 16:18 was never interpreted in a juridical sense, but only *"spiritually."* It was
seen as an assertion of the constitutive significance of *faith*
for the Church, as this is expressed in Peter's confession of
Christ in Mt. 16:16: "You are the Christ, the Son of the
living God." Two examples must suffice. The Alexandrian
theologian *Origen* (d. 254) comments after citing Mt. 16:18:
"But the rock is every disciple of Christ."[26] *John Chrysostom*
(d. 407) explains: "You are Peter, and upon this rock I will
build my Church, that is to say, *upon the faith which you
have confessed."*[27] The idea of primacy *could not* have come
about on the basis of the New Testament passages concerning Peter, not against the background of this kind of exegesis.

In the *Latin West,* too, the spiritual interpretation was the
prevailing one. Although *Ambrose* of Milan (d. 397) believed
that the Roman community had a central position in the
Church, he was still unwilling to admit any juridical primacy
founded on Mt. 16:18. *Peter stands for the Church.*[28] Ambrose even shows resistance to Roman claims when he says,
yes, Peter has a "primacy of confession, not of honor, a primacy of faith, not of procedure."[29] In the same vein, *Augustine* says: "What the Church possesses from Christ as its own,
Peter represents allegorically and tangibly. *Accordingly 'Rock'*

stands as allegory for the Church."[30]

But there was also a juridical interpretation of Mt. 16:18 in the Western Church. North African theologians in particular were strongly inclined to a legal bent of mind. They interpreted this passage to mean Peter's appointment to the leadership of the Church and cited it in order to establish *episcopal* power. It is at least doubtful that Rome motivated its own claim with this kind of theological reasoning as early as the third century, although the Roman bishop, Stephen I, may perhaps have argued in such a fashion.

Tertullian (d. after 220), a North African jurist theologian, polemicized against an unnamed bishop who had supported his opinions and edicts concerning the sacrament of penance with a reference to Mt. 16:18. Tertullian answers him: "If, because the Lord has said to Peter, 'Upon this rock I will build my Church . . .' or 'Whatsoever you shall have bound or loosed on earth . . .' you therefore presume that the power of binding and loosing has come down to you, that is, to every church related to Peter, how can you be so bold as to frustrate and distort the clear intention of the Lord who conferred this gift *personally on Peter?*"[31]

This text used to be applied to the *Roman* bishop and was counted as proof that Rome had laid a *theological* claim to primacy at this early date. Today it is generally recognized that the bishop under attack here was the bishop of Carthage who had been appealing to Mt. 16:18 in order to shore up his episcopal authority over his own community.[32] Thus an interpretation of Mt. 16:18 in the sense of a Roman primacy cannot be discerned here either. Even so, both the bishop in question *and* Tertullian understood this passage to mean the *juridical* fulness of adminstrative power. The bishop thought it to mean the foundation of every episcopal office; Tertullian understood it to be the foundation of a non-transferable primacy of Peter. This juridical interpretation of Mt. 16:18 provided the matrix out of which Rome could adopt the passage to suit its own purposes, but this only happened later.

A further step in that direction was taken by *Cyprian,* bishop of Carthage (d. 258). In his *Epistle 33,* he interprets Mt. 16:18 in a juridical sense to mean the foundation of *episcopal* power, specifically that of *all* bishops. In his book *About the Unity of the Church* (4), Cyprian writes: "The primacy is given to Peter." If we take a close look at this passage, however, is becomes clear that Cyprian understood this primacy solely in a *temporal* sense. Peter was the *first* (Apostle) to receive the power of binding and loosing. Afterwards this same power was transmitted to *all* the Apostles. So, too, today all bishops possess *one* and the *same* office and so, too, in the conduct of their dioceses they are responsible *only to God* (*Epistle* 59). Cyprian makes this point even more emphatic in a second edition of this same book, probably in opposition to Roman claims. The interpretation of Karl Baus is correct on this point: "Closer analysis of Cyprian's linguistic usage obliges us to abandon these texts as conclusive proofs that the idea of the Roman primacy existed in the mind of the North African bishop."[33]

This question became important in the so-called *heretical baptism controversy.* At issue was the question whether Christians who had been baptized by heretics had to be rebaptized when they entered the Catholic Church. The churches at Carthage (*Cyprian*) and in Asia Minor were in favor of rebaptizing. Rome, on the other hand, made a plea for the validity of the baptism already conferred. In the course of this argumentation the Roman bishop, Stephen I (254-257), seems to have appealed to Mt. 16:18. We gather this from the polemical reaction of Bishop *Firmilian* of Caesarea in Asia Minor (preserved by *Cyprian* in *Epistle* 75). Firmilian writes: "Stephen glories in his position as a bishop and claims to hold succession to Peter" (*Epist.* 75:12). This citation always used to be taken as evidence that, for the first time in history, Stephen I had made the appeal to Peter in order theologically to support his title to leadership in the Church. However, this interpretation may well be wrong. At least Firmilian was not at all polemicizing against this assertion; he himself did not even take it to mean a claim to primacy. His criticism was directed rather at Stephen's attitude toward the question of the heretics' baptism: Stephen exhibits a *manifesta stultitia!* The stupidity to which Firmilian refers "is that one who claims to be the successor to the foundation of the foundations should accord the status of church to heretical groups. It is not the Petrine claim, but the failure to measure up to it that outrages Firmilian. Indeed, it would appear that Firmilian did not understand that claim as having any definable juris-dictional consequences."[34]

It would thus seem that Stephen indeed used Mt. 16:18 in the sense of the North African interpretation in order to shore up his own position with respect to the members of his own community. However, *Cyprian's* behavior seems to in-dicate that perhaps Stephen did after all argue in the sense of a theological claim to primacy. In order to exclude any misunderstanding about the independence of the episcopacy from Rome, Cyprian subsequently revised a chapter of his book *On the Unity of the Church.*

Stephen later refused to receive Cyprian's delegation in Rome when it brought the decisions of some North African synods concerning re-baptism. Karl Baus considers this to be "the most important demonstration of Rome's position of preeminence yet undertaken by one of its bishops."[35] This conclusion is completely unwarranted. Stephen's action is rather more a matter of the misbehavior of an obdurate man. In any event, the theological appeal to Peter in support of the Roman position of prominence plays no further role for the next hundred years. At least it cannot be documented. Not until Pope *Damasus* (366-384), at a moment when the trend of the time had favored an increased significance for

Rome, do we find a pope laying theological claim to Peter as the foundation for his own office.[36]

Chapter Three

From Constantine to the Mass Migrations

The period of history examined here is extremely complex. We must refrain from a detailed and extensive presentation and only mention briefly a few points that are important for our topic.

A. The Significance of the Constantinian Turning-point

The political developments in the fourth century reinforced the influence of the Roman bishop in the Church. Especially in the Western part of the Empire, Rome became the dominating influence. This position of prominence received conclusive theological underpinnings under Pope Damasus I.

1. Through the Convention of Milan in 313, the Church became politically free in the Roman Empire and soon became a determining factor in its public life. Many of the privileges hitherto reserved to the heathen religions now passed over to the Church; her bishops inherited the legal public status which the heathen priests had enjoyed in the Roman State. Finally, toward the end of the century, under Emperor *Theodosius* (d. 395), Christianity became the official state religion.

As a result of the "Constantinian turning-point," for the first time the Church was in a position to operate largely unrestricted throughout the whole Empire and even to settle and regulate conflicts. The Roman community was predestined precisely for such large-scale activity. The churches in the Latin West in particular had very little experience in this area, and so they readily agreed to leave the initiative to the more cosmopolitan Rome. "Gradually Rome developed into the undisputed premier see of the West, and the one which dealt with the East on behalf of the West."[1]

2.   The emperor *Constantine* transferred his residence to Constantinople and built up the city in a rich way. This gave new impetus to a development which had begun earlier. East and West each developed more and more its own importance and thus sowed the seed for their later separation. The removal of the imperial residence from Rome also had the effect of engendering in Constantinople a community whose bishops soon made rival claims vis-a-vis those of the Roman bishop.

Constantine had given the imperial Lateran Palace as a gift to the Roman bishop. From then on the Roman bishop resided there; this served to enhance his prestige in the eyes of the people. In particular, the bishop of Rome was now out from under the immediate influence of the Emperor. This fact became very important under the Christian Emperors.

In this way, Rome became even more of a religious center. In addition, during the period of the decline of the Roman Empire, the Roman bishop also became a political factor contributing to the maintenance of order in the Western half of the Empire.

3.   As the Church and the Empire came to be coextensive geographically, Christianity gradually took over the administrative forms of the Empire: the city, the province, and, from the fourth century on, the diocese. Parallel to this development and more clearly in the East than in the West, the Church adopted already existing transregional structures. Cities became dioceses of a single bishop, with the surrounding countryside belonging to his jurisdiction. Church provinces were established around a metropolis or central city, and a metropolitan bishop had a certain supervisory power over the bishops of his province. In the East, super church centers,

the Patriarchates, arose along parallel lines with the dioceses of the Empire. By and large, these were old apostolic churches whose influence reached far beyond the boundaries of a province—here too later development derived from earlier beginnings. Especially noteworthy were Antioch in Syria and Alexandria in Egypt; soon Constantinople and Jerusalem became equally significant. In the West, there were no such large-scale divisions. Rome *alone* was considered to be the Patriarchate of the West; even here, however, there were occasional problems of jurisdiction with Carthage and Milan.

4.   This background is needed to understand further developments in regard to the importance of Rome. In 314, a *Synod of Arles* informed the Roman bishop of its decrees "so that everyone will know what they have to observe in the future." Rome was the center of information and the disperser of news.

In 335, the Roman bishop, Julius I, declared invalid a decision of the *Synod of Tyros*. While recognizing Rome's precedence in Canons 3-5, at a *Synod in Sardika* in 343, the Eastern Church rejected this annulment. In 418 a *Council of Carthage* even forbade any appeal to Rome.

At the *Ecumenical Council of Constantinople* in 381, Rome was conceded a priority of *honor;* but at the same time it was demanded that Constantinople be the second in rank. "The basis on which the Easterners would seem to be acting would be the assumption that church organizations should parallel the organization of society."[2] The self-confident Roman bishop, *Damasus I,* rose up in opposition to this claim. At a Roman Synod in 382, he argued against Constantinople that its claim rested solely on *political* motivation. Rome's precedence, however, was not political and was not first established through synodal decrees. After citing the "Rock" pericope (Mt. 16:18), he contended that "thus the Roman Church is the premier see of the Apostle Peter..."[3] Second and third in rank are Alexandria (said to be founded by

Peter's disciple Mark!) and Antioch (where *Peter* resided for a time!).

Although some arguments indicate that Stephan I thought the same way (see above, p. 33 f.), this is the first time that it can be established with historical certainty that a *theological justification* for a universal Roman primacy is given by referring to Mt. 16:18. Thus the justification of papal primacy used by Vatican I with reference to Peter appears in the history of Rome for the first time conceivably with Stephan I in the middle of the third century and, for certain, with Damasus I in 383. It is clear that this theological rationale is used to justify a factual power position which already existed. The theological justification is intended to consolidate that position and establish it on a firm and universal footing.

5. A glance at the great theologians of the time indicates just how little this *theological* claim was recognized outside Rome, even though Rome enjoyed a certain practical ecclesiastical importance. Rome's claim was never recognized in the East. While it is true that a certain kind of "primacy" was granted to the Roman Church because of its location in the old capital, this "primacy" was not understood in the sense of Rome's interpretation.[4]

At the beginning of this period, the situation was not very different in the *West*. The opinions of Damasus were supported by some theologians, such as his friend *Jerome,* and *Optatus of Mileve.* But others, like *Ambrose* and *Augustine* (see above, p. 34 f.), rejected this theology. Nevertheless, Augustine, for whom the "rock-man," Peter, was an allegory of the Church, did a great deal to promote the development of the primacy. His idea of the Church became more and more authoritative in his polemics against "heretics," opposing all false compassion for them. In arguing against them, he placed great value on the ancient tradition, on the succession of the Roman bishops from Peter, and on official Church decisions.

But *one* statment of his in particular made history. In *Sermo 131:10,* Augustine attacks a heresy which two African Councils had already rejected. They had sent a delegation to Rome, and Rome had already sent its afirmative response. Augustine says: "The matter is settled—*causa finita est.* Would that the error would simply cease to exist!"[5] Later this phrase was to become *"Roma locuta, causa finita"*— when Rome has decided, the matter is settled.

However, Augustine did not mean to say that something is settled by Roman judgment. The speaker in this sermon is a learned theologian *and* "authoritarian" Church leader weary of endless controversy with erroneous theories. Theologically, he wants to say, everything is clear. Two Councils have passed judgment, and Rome, too, has taken a stand in the matter. If only this would suffice for the whole affair to be over and done with at long last! Augustine is not testifying to any absolute doctrinal competence on the part of Rome, but only to the fact that theology and the Church have now weathered the storm created by all this erroneuos teaching.

Nonetheless, in the subsequent period a gradual recognition of Rome's theological claim developed in the West. "It was gradually accepted in the West as the basis for Rome's already very real leadership."[6]

B. The Position of the Bishops of Rome in the Declining Western Empire

As a result of the increasing weakness within the Western Roman Empire in the fifth century, the bishops of Rome became in instrument for the promotion of order in society far beyond the realm of the Church itself. Self-confidently they demanded the recognition of the priority of their position within the Church. However, this priority still cannot be compared with a contemporary primacy of jurisdiction. This episcopal claim was a religious prolongation of the imperial

Roman tradition.

1. More and more the Roman bishop assumed the function of a "bankruptcy administrator of the Roman Empire" in the West. "During the crisis created by the mass migrations, the Roman bishops frequently proved to be the mainstay of their people, and this circumstance greatly enhanced their prestige."[7] In this way they made their entry into "mainstream politics." *Innocent I* (401-417) sought to attain an equilibrium between the Roman Emperor in the East and the Western Goth, King Alaric. *Leo I* (440-461) managed to save both Rome and Northern Italy from pillage by negotiating with the Hun chieftan, Attila, and the Vandal king, Geiseric.

2. In order to consolidate the Roman claim, the conceptions of the Church as the "Body of Christ" under Christ as its "Head" were adopted from the Epistles to the Ephesians and to the Colossians. The Roman community was understood to be the head of the Body of Christ. In this way, the political role of the city of Rome during the time of the Roman Empire was translated into Christian language. Perhaps one could better say, *Christianity adapted Roman political thought to its own purposes.* "Thus the features of the office of Peter came to correspond more to the political world and the social order of Roman antiquity than to the conception of the New Testament *diakonia.*"[8]

The Roman bishop, *Innocent I* (401-417), therefore, took it upon himself to feel "anxiety for all the churches" (2 Cor. 11:28).[9] From imperial usage, *Boniface I* (417-422) adopted the notion of *principatus* and applied it to his own function.[10] He designated Rome "the head of all the churches."[11] Against the Nestorian "heresy," *Celestine I* (422-432) emphasized that what Rome says is decisive for whoever belongs to the Church community; and at a Roman synod he excluded Nestorius from the Church. Needless to say, such an action involves a definite claim to teaching authority, but it is a claim which always seems to be bound up with church "political" competence. But we cannot conclude from this fact that "Celestine was claiming full *teaching authority* and that the absolute character of this authority emerges clearly from the fact that the sentence passed ... was regarded as the 'judgment of Jesus Christ himself.' "[12] This is no longer an interpretation of history. It amounts to an interpretation which projects today's Church law back into history.

Leo I, the Great (440-461), developed the idea of papal primacy to an initial culmination. A self-assured man who was also active in the political arena, Leo saw himself as wholly an heir to the Petrine rock-function (*Sermo* 5:4). It was from Peter that the Apostles had received their power. Peter and his successors have priority over all other bishops. Leo the Great is the first one clearly to formulate the legal conception of papal primacy. As the *legal* successors of Peter, the bishops of Rome have at the same time a universal primacy, that is, the *fulness of power* (*plenitudo potestatis*) in the Church. Notwithstanding their New Testament vocabulary, the images which Leo used to establish the Roman primacy derive from "the consciousness of imperial Rome."[13] In a sermon in honor of Saints Peter and Paul, Leo praised the city of Rome in these words: "These [Peter and Paul] are the ones who have brought you to such fame ... You, Rome, should expand your dominion through divine religion even further than you did before through worldly might" (*Sermo* 82:1).[14]

Leo managed to increase his prestige to a certain extent even in the Eastern part of the Church. During the lengthy Christological controversies, Rome had cut a good figure and appeared as the haven of orthodoxy. In addition, Leo was no mean theologian. His doctrinal treatise concerning the divine and human natures of Christ was read before the Patriarch of Constantinople at the (fourth) Ecumenical Council of Chalcedon in 451. On hearing it, the Council Fathers broke into spontaneous acclamation and called out, "Peter has spoken through Leo!"

Of course, this acclamation cannot be taken to mean a general recognition of the Roman primacy. Leo's treatise was in no way decisive for the matter before the Council: its reading was followed by intensive debates. Even Leo recognized that it required the confirmation of the Council Fathers. A jurisdictional primacy such as we know it today was hardly conceivable at that time. Even for Leo himself, the bishops are independent leaders of their own dioceses, although in his conception they possess their episcopal dignity through sharing in the office of Peter. Characteristically, it is only the Vicar of Thessalonika, whom Leo had appointed himself, that he handled like some kind of functionary.

3. In the fourth and fifth centuries, the Roman bishops acquired their highly important role virtually without effort on their own part. But it was no accident that the popes' first "imperial" claims coincided historically with the crisis in the Western Roman Empire. The Roman bishops were heirs to a conception of empire which they applied to religion.

The vacuum of power in the West which they filled was due to a number of factors: the disappearance of the pagan priesthood, the absence of any tradition of church history in the West, the weakness of the Western Roman Emperor, and the convulsions caused by the mass migrations of peoples. The Roman bishops recognized this vacuum, and they acted accordingly. As bishops of the capital city and the only apostolic Church in the West, they possessed unique opportunities; and they took advantage of them. To reproach them for this would be foolish and lacking in a sense of history. Somebody had to fill the vacuum. "Clearly this process occurred under the impact of historical circumstances and one can rightfully ask whether the Roman bishops were not forced to make this often very concrete interpretation (of their task) in order to respond to the historical exigencies."[15]

P. Stockmeier is correct in pointing out that the Roman

bishops acted with an "often amazing lack of concern" when they surrounded themselves "with worldly trappings" and expressed their claim in pagan concepts. "Thus in some respects, such as its monarchical form, the appearance of the office of Peter resembled the former emperor more than the biblical image of Peter."[16]

4. The theological justification of the papal claim to power by apealing to Peter's primacy cannot but appear to be an *a posteriori* Christian superstructure built on the actual exigencies of the times. But this attempt to justify specific actions by the Bible should not be viewed exclusively in a negative light. It may involve misusing Scripture by interpreting it in an opportunistic way; however, the Roman bishops were probably convinced that, in taking advantage of the opportunities presented by historical circumstance, their activity in the Church and in the world was a part of *their* Christian duty.

5. Naturally, the *claim* to a fairly universal primacy did not correspond to the reality. Ever since the time of Damasus, and even more so since Leo, the extent of the claim was far greater than that of its actual recognition. This was true especially for the East, but also, by and large, for the West. Clearly the impression which their own narrower horizon of experience made on them had its effect on the way these Roman bishops expressed their claim to primacy. Inspired by the tradition of imperial Rome, they generalized their role in the North Italian and Western Church generally and overinterpreted its occasional confirmation on a more global scale, as at the Council of Chalcedon in 451. It is the same kind of overestimation one observes in other univeralistic claims, for example, the "most Christian king," the "king of kings."

Evidence for the designation of the Roman bishop as *"Pope"*—from the Greek *pappas* = father—is found for the first time in Rome in the second half of the fourth century. Originally it was a form of address for abbots, bishops, and

Patriarchs in the East. Since the middle of the fifth century, it was used predominantly as a title for Patriarchs. The titles *pontifex maximus* and *vicar of Christ* came into usage in the early and high Middle Ages. *Pontifex maximus* was formerly the title of honor for the Roman pagan high priest.[17]

Chapter Four

Papal Primacy
in the Early Middle Ages

At the close of antiquity, the foundations were laid for the development of a Roman primacy. These foundations were the actual importance of the Roman bishop, especially in the West, and, in addition, a theological claim to succession to the primacy of Peter. The issue in the period following was to obtain a hearing for this claim. The Roman bishops succeeded in this effort during the course of a series of political and ecclesiastical developments. In this chapter we shall sketch summarily the most important stages on the way to consolidating papal primacy as well as the alterations occurring in the conception itself.

A. From the Collapse of the Western Empire to the Beginning of the Islamic Mission

The Christian mission to the Germans and the Islamic expeditions of conquest both strengthened the central position of Rome in the Western Church.

1. During the course of the fifth century, the Roman Empire was increasingly convulsed by the expanding conquests of the Germanic tribes. In the territory that used to belong to the Empire a series of statelike structures arose in which a numerically small number of Germans ruled a much larger population. For the most part the Germanic tribes knew only the Arian form of Christiainty. Consequently it was through contact with Rome that the bulk of the "Catholic" population and its bishops sought to keep in touch with the rest

of Catholic Christianity. However, this orientation toward Rome did not stand in the way of the erection of self-governing local national churches.

2. *One* important Germanic tribe, the Franks, adopted the Catholic form of Christianity from the beginning. Their chieftain, Clovis, was baptized in 496 in Rheims. But the church in the kingdoms set up by the Franks was a kind of national church which had no recognizable attachment to Rome.

3. The importance of the Roman bishop as a stabilizing factor during this period of turmoil became even greater. As a result, Bishop *Gelasius I* (492-496) became the first Pope who could propose the so-called doctrine of the two powers. He claimed for himself "full power to make laws in the Church." Up to this time, only synods could appoint statutes of law over and beyond existing legal traditions. Gelasius "was the first pope to add his decretals and those of his predecessors to the synodal collections of canons. He attributed a legislative power to these similar to that of the synodal resolutions."[1] However, this development had not yet gone so far as to make it possible for papal rights to abrogate the rest of church law. "The popes too have always regarded themselves as bound by the conciliar canons and they have always promised on election to respect these canons and the practices of the whole Church." Nevertheless, ever since then, papal decretals have formed an integral part of the canon law of the Western Church.[2]

4. In the unruly time which followed, the whole Latin West was divided into numerous small kingdoms with flexible boundaries. One figure in particular is noteworthy in this period, *Gregory I*, the Great (590-604). Gregory the Great was the first Pope to adopt the title *servus servorum Dei*— the servant of the servants of God. With full deliberation, but without much success, he sought to group the many more or less autonomous national churches around the Church at

Rome. At least in the religious sphere he wanted to implement the old idea of the empire. It was perfectly evident to him that "that man belongs to the Church who stands in union with Rome."[3]

In 553, the Eastern Roman Emperor, *Justinian,* "liberated" Italy from the Arian Goths. In Ravenna, in Northern Italy, he appointed a political governor for the West. This institution lasted until 753.

During the time of Gregory, however, Rome was threatened once more by the Longobards. In such conflicts it was the Roman bishop who acted as representative of the Eastern Roman Emperor; hardly ever did the governor in Ravenna do so.

Gregory initiated two developments which are important for later history. He reformed the numerous properties belonging to the Roman community, the so-called *Patrimonium Petri,* or inheritance of Peter. This reform led to the economic prosperity of Rome and laid the groundwork for what later became the Papal States. Further, in 596 Gregory, himself a former Benedictine monk, sent forty Benedictines under the leadership of Abbot Augustine to England. As a result, "the English church later honored him as its founder."[4]

This initiative was the first Rome had taken with regard to the missions, and it proved momentous for the future. In retrospect, Rome thus came to be seen as a "missionary center." Furthermore, as a result, the English church was strongly Rome-oriented from its very beginning. Gregory himself had never conceived of taking England under his own immediate sovereignty. Instead, he turned it over to the jurisdiction of the bishop of Arles. "If he had had his way, England would have become only a new province of the Gallo-Frankish church, and the Roman influence there would have been scarcely any greater than on the continent." Only because Gregory's successors later continued their missionary activity without Frankish assistance did this first Roman initiative become the "turning point .. which had such decisive importance for the development of the papacy."[5]

Johannes Haller (d. 1947) saw in the Rome-fixation of the Anglo-Saxon church the historic turning point in the history of the papacy. For it was this church whose later missionary activity was to tie Middle and Western Europe to the papacy (see below, Chap. 4-C). Though it is too one-sided and exclusive, this thesis does bring out an essential aspect of the matter.

Two factors in particular brought about the crystallization of the ever greater orientation of the English toward Rome. First, there was the Roman initiative in estabilshing and consolidating the English church and, second, there was the Germanic *devotion to Peter*. This strong predilection for the figure of Peter honored the keeper of the gates of heaven and the manly prince of the Apostles who could even take up the sword on occasion (see below, Chap. 4-C).

5. The appearance of Islam and its dynamic expansion in the seventh and eighth centuries further diminished the power of the Eastern Roman Emperor. As a consequence, the governor in Ravenna was also less and less in a position to carry out the imperial will in the West. The Roman bishops sought to fill the resulting vacuum of power by initiating more and more activities of their own. The loss of North Africa to Islam and the threat to Spain—in 711 the kingdom there collapsed—forced the endangered churches to seek protection against Arab invasion. They appealed for help outside their own borders, and so the influence of Rome became stronger still.

B. Loss of Church Unity between East and West

The churches in the East and in the West became more and more estranged from one another. Progressive alienation finally led to a complete break. This cleared the way for Rome definitively to consolidate its dominion in the West.

No other church could now counter the Roman claim by recourse to its own ancient apostolic tradition.

1. For the cultivated Greeks in the East, the new world of the barbarian Germans was largely incomprehensible. But Rome necessarily had to come to terms with this world. Thus in the following period the two halves of the Church became more and more estranged. Knowledge about each other and mutual communication were restricted to a bare minimum.

2. Smaller controversies had already occurred in the seventh century. But in the eighth and ninth centuries, the *iconoclast controversy* produced the first break between the Roman bishop and the official policy of the Eastern Church, though this was not yet a formal rupture of their relationship. Rome objected to the imperial prohibition of the veneration of images of the saints. The situation remained tense until 843 when the Empress *Theodora* solemnly reinstated the veneration of images on the "Feast of Orthodoxy." However, other disputes under Patriarch *Photius* of Constantinople led in 857 to a temporary formal "schism"— a Greek word for the official separation of the two Churches.

3. By the eleventh century the point of no return had been reached. The two halves of the Church had become so completely estranged that it no longer required a major occasion to produce the official break. Such theological controversies as the question of the marriage of priests, the Saturday fast in Lent, the problem of leavened or unleavened bread in the celebration of the Eucharist, the question whether the Holy Spirit proceeds from the Father *through* the Son or from the Father *and* the Son, served both sides as justification for the definitive schism.

In 1053, the Patriarch of Constantinople, *Michael Caerularius,* ordered that all Latin churches and cloisters in Constantinople must convert to the Greek rite. In 1054, papal legates under the direction of the narrow-minded and arrogant *Hum-*

bert of Silva Candida laid on the altar of Hagia Sophia a papal bull of excommunication against the Patriarch of Constantinople.

4. From that point, on the question of restoring church unity hung in the air. Several initiatives were taken, but without result. Earnest attempts to restore unity did not occur until the first half of the fifteenth century, when the Eastern Emperor was threatened once again by the Turks and was forced to seek help in the West from the pope. At the *Council of Union in Ferrara-Florence* (1438-39), under strong pressure from the Emperor, the Greek bishops voted in favor of a decree of union. But this decree was never implemented. Even during the voyage home many of the bishops revoked their consent. In 1453, Constantinople fell to the Turks and the history of the Eastern Empire came to an end. Since that time, the churches of the East have been living under Islamic rule cut off from the Western world.

C. The Anglo-Saxon Mission

Anglo-Saxon missionaries reorganized and reformed the Frankish church. In this way they brought to the continent their veneration of Peter and their ties to Rome.

1. The majority of the Germanic tribes north of the Alps had already been christianized before the eighth century, in particular through the missionary efforts of Irish and Scottish monks. This mission did not produce a unified church organization for the whole geographical area. But it did serve to inculcate everywhere devotion to Peter. "The Irish, too, were devotees of the prince of the Apostles and looked to Rome with reverence and awe."[6]

2. The Anglo-Saxon Mission also undertook to organize institutional church structures. The most important figure in this effort was *Winfrid* (d. 754). With his background of Anglo-Saxon loyalty to Rome, Winfrid saw himself as an envoy of Rome. On his first trip to Rome in 719, he received

an official mission to Germany from *Gregory II*. With the mission he received a new name, *Boniface,* to indicate that from then on he was another person; he had become the Pope's man. On his second trip to Rome in 722, when he was consecrated bishop, Boniface swore allegiance to the Pope, something which only the suburban bishops of Rome had done up to this time. "Thus the missionary bishopric of Boniface was tightly bound to Rome."[7]

At several Frankish councils, Boniface sought to push through his conceptions concerning reform. Thus, as J. Haller summarizes this devolpment, "the Frankish church submitted to Rome and bound itself to Rome."[8] But as far as jurisdictional and organizational aspects are concerned, one should not overestimate this bond. The principle of the local national church had not yet been decisively overcome.[9]

3.   Nonetheless, the allegiance of the Frankish church to the Roman bishops proved decisive for the further development of the papacy. Other factors, such as the substitution of the Roman liturgy for the Frankish liturgy in the mother tongue toward the end of the eighth century, soon strengthened this adherence to Rome. This constituted a breakthrough for the first time toward an "organizational" association of national churches with Rome. At this point the process was only just beginning. But this "organizational" affiliation was supported by the religious and emotional strength of the Germanic Peter-mysticism. Being a Christian and being loyal to the keeper of the keys and his successors were intimately connected from now on in the feelings of the Germans.[10] Charlemagne, for example, was proud of the fact "that the Church in his kingdom had never strayed from the *sancta et veneranda communio*—the sacred and venerable communion—with Rome."[11] However, such statements should not be overestimated. "In his [Charlemagne's] view, the bishop of Rome was really little more than the most important bishop in his empire."[12]

D. Rome's Reliance on the Franks. The Foundation of the Papal States.

Growing estrangement between the Eastern and the Western Church led very early to a narrowing of Rome's orientation toward the West. In the eighth century, Rome's reliance on the Farnks strengthened the religious prestige of the Roman bishops in the West and led to the foundation of the Papal States.

1. In the struggle against the iconoclastic fanaticism of the Eastern Emperor (see above, Chap. 4-B, 2.), the Roman bishop sought to obtain the support of the Franks. In 751, Pope *Zacharias* recognized the legitimacy of the overthrow of the Merovingian kings and the accession to power of the Carolingians with the crowning of Pepin as king. This step made the Pope appear to have the final decision in moral-religious issues on the political scene. In gratitude, Pepin promised the Pope civil jurisdiction over Rome and over the areas of Northern Italy still under the dominion of the Longobards. These were principally areas which until then had been subject directly to the Eastern Empire's governor in Ravenna. Later, after Charlemagne had conquered the Longobard kingdom in 774, the Pope actually took possession of these areas.

2. This act has become known as the "donation of Pepin," although it is disputed whether the territories involved were actually "donated" to the Pope. Nevertheless, this act and its later confirmation by Charlemagne brought about the foundation of the so-called *Papal States,* and thereby initiated a fateful historical development. This church-state lasted until 1870, and even today continues to exist in certain symbolic remnants. Its effect has been to ensnare the Pope definitively in the intricacies of mainstream politics. However, historically it also gave the papacy necessary political freedom and autonomy. "That the Roman Church was able to assert its political freedom is due in the first place to the Papal States."[13] This made it possible in later times for the Pope to intervene wherever political forces were endangering the ecclesiastical freedom of a local national church. Against secular encroachments, oppressed local churches turned to Rome for support.

3. It may have been a consequence of the foundation of the Papal States that the idea of a "Constantinian donation" —*donatio Constantini*—arose in the papal chanceries. According to this notion, the Roman Emperor Constantine is said to have relinquished the Western part of his empire to the current Pope *Silvester*.[14] However, this opinion did not become politically relevant until the High Middle Ages, at which time the "donation" was thought to be genuine. It was not until the fifteenth century that Bishop *Nicholas of Cusa* and others discovered that it was a forgery.

E. Pope Nicholas I

In the ninth century with Pope Nicholas I (d. 867), a highpoint was reached in the centralistic claim of the papacy.

1. Nicholas I attempted to exert even greater influence on the local Frankish church. He intervened in the marriage affairs of King Lothar II and made him subject to his own religious authority. "This centralization of the authority in himself as Pope was, of course, seriously criticized; and he was accused of behaving like an emperor. But he was so determined to put his view of the supreme value of the papacy as the head of the Church's hierarchy into practice that he forced the Bulgarian Church, which had hitherto been quite prepared to join the Western Church, into an alliance with Constantinople."[15]

2. Nicholas insisted on the Church's independence from secular influences. Before him no one had advocated with such clarity Rome's jurisdictional claim—what Congar has called the "juristical authority of Rome." "Conciliar resolu-

tions, for example, were not valid until they had been ratified by Rome. Rome could conclude all legal proceedings and was the supreme court of appeal in the Christian world. The Pope was able to proclaim new laws whenever the occasion demanded it."[16]

3. The *Pseudo-Isidorian Decretals* also orginated in the area of the Frankish church. They emphasize very clearly the primacy of Rome over synods and metropolitans. Probably they were intended to protect suffragan bishops from the encroachments of nearby ecclesiastical and political sovereigns through emphasizing the importance of far-off Rome. That they were so close in spirit to the ideas of Nicholas I surely facilitated the perpetration of the forgery. Their "influence was, however, not really felt until the eleventh century, when it permeated the Church by way of the various collections of ecclesiastical laws."[17]

Chapter Five

Papal Primacy
after the Gregorian Reform

A. The Gregorian Reform

The formation of supraregional church structures and the extension of the influence of the papacy were facilitated in the High Middle Ages by the rise of a universal European culture.
1. A cultural and religious resurgence had been going on in the West since the eleventh century. More and more the Occident came to understand itself as a unity. In terms of this sense of unity, the previous church structures characterized by particularism and individual church organizations were an anachronism. Religious and theological movements were transcending the boundaries of the different regions comprising the entire Western church.

As a result, forms of "universal" or "central" organization became indispensable. Cloisters, for example, which until this time had been self-sufficient and autonomous, began to join together, at first as congregations around central reform cloisters such as Cluny and Gorze. Later on, in the twelfth century, they formed into organized societies like the Cistercians and others. Soon after, in the thirteenth century, centrally administered Orders arose of which the mendicant Orders are the foremost example.

The social stratification of the population, too, displayed similar features across the entire continent. Chivalry provided a basis which was soon strong enough to carry out "European" undertakings—the Crusades. Since the time of the Crusades, neither commerce nor the movements of pilgrims were restricted to "national" boundaries.

2. The papacy used the dynamism of such supraregional, large-scale activity to its own advantage. The history of the Roman Church already disposed its bishops to this task. Both in the religious renewal and in the political activity of the Western church, the Roman bishops emerged stronger than ever before as leaders of the entire Church. A series of popes working in this direction made Rome more and more the center of the Church in the West.

Often with the support of the Cluniac reform movement, they fought for the spiritual renewal of the Church under the banner *libertas ecclesiae*—the freedom of the Church. This implied for them the emancipation of the Church from secular power. Here we can see the first hint of the later distinction and separation of "Church and State"; up to this time both Church and State had been indissolubly intertwined. *Libertas ecclesiae* meant concretely the struggle against simony—the purchase of Church offices, against lay investiture—appointment of clerics to their offices by secular powers, and against the marriage of clerics. Opposition to the latter was based on the fact that married clerics must necessarily use Church goods for the support of their families.

As early as the time of Leo IX, in the middle of the eleventh century, the Roman College of Cardinals developed into a corporate body which assisted the Pope in the government of the universal Church. Until that time the Cardinals had served predominantly liturgical functions. In 1058, *Nicholas II* granted them the exclusive right to elect the Pope.

Gregory VII was an integral part of this development. His theses on the function of the Pope did not initiate revolutionary changes in the prevailing situation, but corroborated traditions already in existence. Consequently, he was only putting into practice the universalistic trends current in the West. Gregory's determination in this matter simply resulted in his finding the first significant formulation for these tendencies.

In 1075, Gregory formulated his conception of the Roman

primacy in the so-called *Dictatus Papae,* which contained twenty-seven principles or guidelines collected from older material. Among these principles are the following. The Pope is the highest political authority; all rulers are required to kiss his foot. He can depose the emperor and dispense his subjects from their allegiance to him. The Roman Church alone is founded by the Lord. (This particular opinion is a negative consequence of the break with the Eastern church: see above, Chap. 4-B.) Only the Pope can promulgate new laws in the Church. Papal decisions have the force of law in the entire Church. The Pope has the right to appoint and depose bishops, to define diocesan boundaries, and so forth.

For the first time in history the claim of the Roman bishop to an immediate primacy of jurisdiction over the whole Church is asserted here in all clarity. "A new phrase became common in the papal documents relating to the Gregorian reform: 'subject to the authority of the apostolic see.' "[2] The legal reservation implied by this clause—*salva auctoritate sedis apostolicae*—was supposed to make it clear that the Pope himself was not bound by the laws. The final decision always belonged to him.

Because of his Peter-mysticism, Gregory was deeply "convinced that no Christian could be saved who was not bound in unity, harmony, and obedience to the representative of Peter."[3]

From this time onward, the conviction grew ever stronger "that the man who was not in agreement with and did not obey the Roman Church was heretical."[4]

3. The Crusades in particular strengthened the leading position of the papacy in the Western Church. The Crusades combined the medieval idea of chivalry and combat with the strong piety of pilgrimages. The papacy set itself at the head of this movement and was thus able to mobilize for its own purposes powerful intellectual, political, and emotional forces transcending every national boundary. Islam, the common ex-

ternal enemy, served to consolidate the Pope's leadership in the West.

4. In the following period, no fundamentally new ideas accrued to the papal claim, but it was formulated more sharply, particularly in its juridical aspects. A series of canonist Popes and papal canonists created a comprehensive papal legislation regulating all areas of Church life. The intention of this legislation was to secure the supremacy of papal might; and the most extreme formulation of this will to power is found in the Bull *unam sanctam* issued by *Boniface VIII* in 1302: "Therefore we declare, state, define, and preach that it is *necessary for salvation for every human creature* to subject himself to the Roman pontiff...."[5]

B. *The Papacy in the Late Middle Ages.*

The might of the papacy continued to develop in the later Middle Ages in spite of all turmoil and setbacks.

1. From 1309 to 1377 the Popes did not reside in Rome, but in Avignon in southern France, where they were subject to the strong influence of the French kings. In spite of this influence, however, precisely during this period a powerful intensification of curial centralism occurred under the banner of papal *plenitudo potestatis*—the fulness of power. The papal treasury system was perfected and papal competence for appointments to numerous Church offices throughout the West was radically extended.[6]

2. Even the subsequent "Western schism" could not essentially diminish Roman might. It did divide the Church into factions supporting different popes and anti-popes and was not resolved until the Council of Constance in 1415. The vexations of this time brought about a strengthening of so-called *conciliarism,* the doctrine of the superiority of an ecumenical council over the Pope. However, the papacy was able to maintain itself through it all.

Not even the profuse religious and moral decadence of the

Renaissance papacy did any extensive damage to Roman might, despite the very bad public image of the papacy it generated. Roman predominance was already too firmly established.

C. The Theory of Papal Infallibility in the Late Middle Ages

The thesis of the Pope's infallibility was formulated for the first time toward the end of the thirteenth century. However, the initial purpose of this theory was NOT to increase the power of the papacy. On the contrary, it was intended to restrict the arbitrariness of papal decisions advocating ever new standpoints and constantly promulgating new laws. As a result, the opinion about papal "infallibility" did not meet with the approval of the Popes.[7]

1. The papal canonists of the twelfth and thirteenth centuries made every effort to extend papal power. Nevertheless, they did not advocate a doctrine of infallibility or even tacitly presuppose it. Rather, they "invariably came to the conclusion that the Pope alone could not provide an adequate guarantee for the stability of that faith."[8] Christ's pledge to Peter that his faith would not waver (Lk. 22:32) "was taken to mean simply that the Church would always survive."[9]

2. The new teaching concerning papal "infallibility" was first propagated within the Franciscan Order. The Franciscans wanted to prevent a later pope from changing a papal decree that was in their own interest. "Thus the purpose of this .. doctrine of infallibility was not to increase the power of future Popes, but to restrict it."[10] (As a matter of fact, in 1323 Pope John XXII revoked and declared heretical a decree of his predecessor that was very dear to one faction within the Franciscan Order.)

3. The opinion did not take hold in the following period. "The idea of papal infallibility was blankly unacceptable even to the most ardent defenders of the Roman see.... The idea was too novel, too radical, too sharply opposed to the juridical conception of papal sovereignty, too alien to the theological tradition of the Church, to command support among respectable theologians."[11]

4. Advocates of papal infallibility such as William of Ockham continued their efforts to restrict the all-too-absolutist gestures of the Popes. But the papal canonists rejected their theories. Only one theologian, *Guido Terreni* (d. 1344), advocated the doctrine of infallibility in a *pro-papal* sense. "However, papal theologians were reluctant to accept Guido's teaching." They did not adopt this teaching until the sixteenth and seventeenth centuries. "But by that time the historical origin of the doctrine of infallibility had been long forgotten."[12]

Chapter Six

Modern Times to the Beginning of the Nineteenth Century

A. The Significance of the Reformation for Papal Primacy

The Reformation was theologically motivated. It sought a reform of the Church on theological grounds. Thus, in a fashion seldom seen before this time, questions of faith became a decisive criterion for the Church. It was precisely the theological opposition to the papacy on the part of the reformers that brought about the need for the Catholic Church to find a theological justification for papal primacy. In the end, the question of papal primacy became a matter of the Confession of Faith. From now on in the Catholic creed, Christian faith and the papacy belonged together.

1.   The end of the Middle Ages was marked by a multiplicity of theological opinions. "The most diverse theological schools, movements, and groups existed alongside one another. Good, but weak, will, and empty phrases, curial superlatives, and radical evangelism created what is for us an unimaginable *theological confusion* about the substance of what it is to be Catholic."[1] Even the Popes of the time "failed to give any leadership in pastoral teaching and instruction."[2] They were not interested in doctrine. They conceived their primacy predominantly from a jurisdictional and political point of view.

With the Reformation this whole situation changed. In a manner unknown since the controversies in the ancient Church about the Trinity and Christology, the question of the right interpretation of the Gospel and the *theological* articles of faith now assumed the forefront of attention. As never before, being a Christian came to mean believing the

right confession of faith. A "confessionalization" and a "the-
ologization" of Christianity took place.

2.   Theological criticism of the papacy—the "whore of Babylon"—already existed at the end of the Middle Ages.[3] The
impulse of the reformers to change Church structures was
in principle "religious" too.[4] They took up the older criticism and helped to make it politically effective. Thus the
absence of hierarchy and papacy in the new "church orders"
of the reformed churches was not only a matter of fact;
these orders were a consequence of *theological* controversy.

3.   In reaction to this controversy in the regions of the Church
which remained Catholic, the papacy became part of the
confession of faith. Catholic was a person who, among other
things, acknowledged the Pope in Rome. This attitude toward
the papacy was a particularly tangible, "political" characteristic of Catholics. In this controversial theological situation,
therefore, it virtually took over the first place of importance
in the creed.

4.   Ever since the Gregorian reform—comparable to the figure
of *Nicholas I* (see above, Chap. 4-E)—the conviction had
grown up that an orthodox Christian must be in union
with the Pope. As a result of the Reformation, however, this
conviction took on a new, *theological* quality. For some since
the Reformation the Pope is an extremely negative figure;
for some, he is even the "Anti-Christ." But for the other side
he is an extremely positive theological figure, the preserver
and cornerstone of the faith.

5.   If anything, this tendency was reinforced by the Scriptura-
sola principle of the Reformation. This principle emphasized Holy Scripture as the sole norm of faith, in sharp
distinction to any papal theological relevance. Thus, in the
Catholic counter-move, Pope, council, and tradition became
all the more important; without them there is no correct
interpretation of Scripture for Catholics. In questions of doctrine, recourse to Rome became customary.

6. The Counter-Reformation was a historical necessity. But just how strongly oriented it was toward the papacy is demonstrated by the *Society of Jesus* founded in 1540. "The members profess the usual three vows. But in addition to these three they take a fourth vow to obey without hesitation —*sine ulla tergiversatione aut excusatione*—every command of the Pope for the salvation of souls and the expansion of the faith."[5] The Jesuit Order has had a decisive influence on Catholic thought in the centuries since its foundation. It has contributed very greatly to establishing obedience to the Pope as a Catholic principle since the Counter-Reformation.

B. The Council of Trent

From this time on, criticism of papal primacy fell under suspicion of heresy. Nevertheless, the conception was still too novel and the self-confidence of the bishops still too strong. Thus the Council of Trent was unable to decide on a definition of the Roman primacy.

1. There were vigorous discussions about the power of the Pope on various occasions during the sessions of the Council of Trent (1545-63). Once the *bishop of Fiesole* criticized a proposal in which the bishops appeared to be the executive organ of the Pope in a particular matter. At this a certain *Bishop Pighino* sprang "to his feet and called out in the direction of the (papal) legates. 'It cannot be tolerated that the bishop of Fiesole attack the Holy See in this matter.' Pighino demanded that the speaker hand over his manuscript so that it could be examined for heresy. The word *heresy* lay in the air . . ."[6]

2. Nevertheless, the accrued rights of the bishops were still so strong that it was as yet of the question to try to arrive at a definition of a universal papal primacy. Episcopalist and Gallican tendencies had not yet been eliminated. The episcopalists advocated the rights of the bishops and the Gallicans the independence of the French church. Hubert Jedin has

written that the Council "sharply distinguished the content of Catholic faith from that of the reformers, though not along the whole line of the controversy. The most bitterly contested doctrinal articles, the definition of the primatial power of the papacy and of the conception of the Church, were still hindered by episcopalist and Gallican tendencies."[7]

C. The Seventeenth and Eighteenth Centuries

The Roman claim to primacy could not be consolidated in the following period either. For a time there was even a decline in the political and ecclesiastical influence of the papacy. There began a "long period of diminished activity."[8] The absolutism of many national governments and, in particular, the strong aspirations of local national churches prevented an all too exclusive development of papal might.

1. Until the beginning of the nineteenth century, the self-confidence of the national churches continued unabated. In France, *Gallicanism,* together with certain Jansenistic currents, restricted any excessive power of the papacy. In Spain, *regalism,* the allegiance of the bishops to the king, took over this protective function. In Austria, *Josephinism,* named after Kaiser Joseph, who intervened very vigorously in the practice and teaching of his church, and in Germany *episcopalism* had the same effect.

Common to all these movements was a steadfast insistence on the autonomy of local national churches and bishops. Basically they all recognized a papal primacy, but all endeavored to keep the actual influence of the papacy within limits. In eighteenth-century France, for example, it was necessary for the validity of a papal bull that it be "accepted by the bishops and registered with the chambers of parliament."[9] On occasion a theological motivation was given for these restrictions of the primatial power. The authority of the Pope was bound to natural law, to the civil law of the Christian nations, and to canon law, the law of the Church.

There were even those who taught the sovereignty of an ecumenical council over the Pope.

2. The most important type of episcopalism in Germany was called *Febronianism*. Under the pseudonym *Justinus Febronius*, the auxiliary bishop of Trier, J. N. *von Hontheim*, published in the years 1763-73 a five-volume work on the state of the Church and the lawful power of the Pope. His purpose in writing was to avoid placing any unnecessary roadblocks in the way to a reunion of Christians. To this end, Hontheim demanded a return to the Church structure of the first century. He advocated the supremacy of the Council over the Pope. In the practice of papal reservations and in the establishing of nunciatures he saw symptoms of decay. And in place of papal monarchy he demanded a plurality of national churches. In order to achieve this goal, people should be instructed in the *history* of the Church. "The result of twenty-three years of diligent work, this excellent book was translated into various languages. . . . In the meantime the eighty-year-old Hontheim was brought by all manner of intimidation to recant. In order to have peace in his advanced age he did so. However, the arguments his book contained lost none of their significance thereby. No one had refuted them."[10]

D. The Thesis of Papal "Infallibility"

From the sixteenth to the eighteenth century, the teaching of a papal "infallibility" was advocated from time to time, particularly in Roman theology. However, this idea did not assume a prominent place, nor was it particularly relevant for the Church.

1. The doctrine of papal "infallibility" was held, for example, by the apologist *Albert Pigge* (d. 1542), some of whose works were even put on the *Index* later.[11] In the sixteenth and seventeenth centuries we find similar conceptions in Roman circles as well.

2.   However, these ideas were theologically irrelevant at that time and also ineffective with respect to Church politics. In early eighteenth-century France, for example, as Louis Cognet observes, "the personal infallibility of the Pope was held by practically none of the French theologians at this time."[12]

Chapter Seven

Breakthrough to
Papal "Absolutism"
in the Nineteenth Century

A. Political Development Favors the Position of the Pope

The definition of a universal primacy of jurisdiction and the definition of papal "infallibility" were possible only because the proud national churches of France and Germany had become disorganized in the aftermath of Napoleonic rule. Furthermore, because of their difficult political situation, the diaspora and mission churches in and outside Europe sought a closer union with Rome.

1. A complete reorganization of ecclesiastical affairs occurred in France under *Napoleon* after the convulsions of the French revolution. In 1801, Napoleon concluded a *Concordat* with Pope Pius VII in which he secured extensive powers for the State. Corresponding to the new organization of civil departments, the French church was divided into sixty bishoprics, including ten archdioceses. For political reasons, Napoleon requested the resignation of the entire existing episcopate.

The Pope agreed to this demand. Thus with a stroke of the pen all the French bishops were dismissed from office. The proud Gallican episcopacy was thereby eliminated while, at the same time. the ecclesiastical power of the Pope was immeasurably increased. Even though the Pope had only acted under pressure from Napoleon, and even though the dismissal was effective only because of Napoleon's power, still the removal of the episcopate of an entire nation was something absolutely new in history. This action altered the perspectives of Church law. Pius VII rightly recognized how much this act would contribute to the acceptance of the distinguished "position of the Pontifex maximus at the head of the Catholic hierarchy."[1]

Concerning this event Ignaz von Döllinger wrote: "When Napoleon discerned the political necessity of reconstituting the French church and negotiated it with Pius VII, Bellarmine [d. 1621, an extremely hierarchical and papal-minded theologian and Cardinal] and the curialist system won so comprehensive a victory that even French curialists had to admit that it was unprecedented.... The Concordat of 1801 meant ... the practical destruction of Gallican freedom, and not only that, but of the Gallican church as well. Newly constituted on the basis of curialism, the French church had to submit to it with increasing consequences. Indeed, a large number of bishops protested against Pius VII's violent action ... but Pius VII had no difficulty in finding enough ambitious individuals willing to fill the vacant episcopal sees."[2]

2. Previously, in 1794, Napoleon had occupied the lands west of the Rhine River in Germany. When he reorganized the territories of the German Empire, Napoleon gave to the German princes the possessions of the Church in the rest of Germany in compensation for his taking over these lands. In 1803, the so-called *Reichsdeputationshauptschluss* (Committee of Deputation for the Empire), an eight-man commission of princes, undertook the distribution of the Church goods. It amounted practically to a complete expropriation of the German church, "which had once been the richest church in Christendom," with 1,700 square miles of land, over three million inhabitants, and a yearly income of around 21,000,000 gulden.[3]

Some genuinely positive results came out of this so-called secularization. Children of noble families, for example, were no longer interested in bishoprics. Men "from the people" interested in doing pastoral work now became bishops. But these positive developments were not without some disadvantages. Catholic bishoprics were reduced to financial and political dependence on princes who were largely Protestant and thought in terms of a state Church; consequently, Catholic bishops sought to safeguard themselves against this dependence by a strong reliance on Rome. Rome alone could guarantee a certain freedom of movement, and it did its best by concluding a number of concordats.

The proud and rich German bishops and the clerical electors were now a thing of the past. Thus, in a second major country besides France, the concept of papal primacy could take strong root and flourish. *Ultramontanism* (from *ultramontain,* i.e., beyond the Alps) became a strong movement in both countries: the support of the Pope was sought in all matters.

3.   Other churches also were forced to seek a tight bond with Rome in this period. "The episcopates of Italy and Spain found the Roman pontiff a natural ally against revolutionary movements engaging in variously aggressive actions against the Church."[4] The churches of the Catholic diaspora also found themselves in difficult straits. In order to maintain themselves to some degree in the face of Protestant majorities and governments, they were forced to seek the Pope's backing. Thus a continous papal influence was created in these churches, in particular in Holland and England. The young "missionary churches" in North America and Asia also had a natural interest in binding themselves closely to Rome.[5] In a certain sense, these churches were born in the cradle of Roman curialism.

B. The "Triumphalist" Movement in Catholicism

From the beginning of the nineteenth century at the latest, Catholicism became increasingly characterized by a conservative and triumphalist trend, not only in theology but in Church affairs and politics as well. The guiding image of Catholicism was that of a Church under the monarchical leadership of the Pope, sharply distinguished from all modern currents of thought. The decrees of Vatican Council I later in the century were only possible because of this thinking.

1. Ever since the end of the sixteenth century, the influence of the Society of Jesus brought about an ever stronger accentuation upon the idea of *authority,* and with an intensity unusual up to this time. An obedient attitude toward Church authority and especially toward the Pope came more and more to be the criterion of a genuine Catholic.

In 1773, Pope *Clement XIV* suppressed the Jesuits because of their entanglement in politics and as a result of severe external pressure. However, the Society was founded again in 1814, and, with renewed vigor, the activities of the Society led to an expansion of the authoritarian church system. Ignaz von Döllinger wrote: "Wherever the Society of Jesus was in control, the system, too, reigned in the form given it in the sixteenth century as the only fully orthodox one."[6]

2. This theological and ecclesiastical movement had an interest in everything concerned with authority and authoritative decisions. In later times, it allied itself with an equally triumphalist-minded political romanticism for which peace and order under the authority willed by God were the highest goals.

a. Inspired by this current of thought, a number of the French laity and clergy could even look forward to a world government by the Pope (!) as the culmination of all their wishes. The philosopher of state, *Joseph de Maistre,* described the Pope in his book *Du pape* as the middle point of a new European monarchical feudal order. There can be "no European religion without Christianity, no Christianity with Catholicism, no Catholicism without the Pope, no Pope without the supremacy that is his due."[7] In addition, de Maistre attributed infallibility to the Pope. Two laymen, *Chateaubriand* and

Bonald, presented similar arguments. Finally, the French priest, *Lamennais,* picked up these ideas and refined them theologically. He too advocated papal infallibility and placed the Pope at the midpoint of Catholic emotions and reflection. The ideas of Lamennais were publicized widely by *Louis Veuillot,* editor of the *Univers.* Just how extreme this movement became is indicated in a remark by the English lay theologian, *W. G. Ward.* Ward said he would gladly have a new encyclical or authoritative interpretation from the Pope with his breakfast each morning.[8]

b. But the "triumphalist" approach to the position of the Pope was also subjected to *theological* criticism. In particular the Catholic Tübingen School in Germany was known for its critical reflection. *Johann Adam Möhler,* for example, granted the singular position of the papacy theologically; but he wanted to eliminate all non-theological argument from this issue.

Nevertheless, "triumphalist" ideas were publicized in Germany, too, in a number of theological "circles" "characteristic of the German Catholic revival at the beginning of the century."[9] Best known are the circles of *Clemens Maria Hofbauer* and *Friedrich Schlegel* in Vienna, and a *Mainz Circle* to which a number of Alsatians also contributed. This latter "circle" in particular engaged in extensive publicity. "They wanted to educate the clergy in a very Roman and anti-Protestant spirit. To this end, they disseminated for seminary instruction and in the popular contributions to their periodical, *The Catholic,* the ultramontane theses of Bellarmine."[10] Other circles also propagated these ideas, with the result that "the ultramontane point of view penetrated into theological education and into the teaching of a number of canonists."[11]

3. Through the reorganization of Europe after the fall of Napoleon, the Popes were once again gaining political prestige. They drew upon these developments and consciously worked toward "the monarchization of the Church."[12] Par-

allel to these efforts, they sought to delineate the sphere of the Church and to protect it from all influences by the spirit of the times. In 1832, *Gregory XVI* (d. 1846) published the Encyclical *Mirari vos* condemning, among other things, liberalism and the heretical advocacy of freedom of conscience and freedom of the press. This encyclical was the first of a chain of reactionary papal statements leading up to the *Syllabus* of Pius IX (see below, Chap. 7-B, 6).[13]

4. Theological higher education was for the most part Church-controlled and, consequently, was readily kept in line. Only in Germany and Austria did an extremely active university theology exist that was to some extent at least independent of Church control. Here theological research critically confronted the spirit of the age by making use of new scientific methods—in particular, historical research. "Since they were not subject to the exclusive control of the bishops, the theological faculties of the state universities, particularly in Germany and Austria, aroused suspicions. Ultramontists wanted to substitute seminaries for them too, and this wish remained a constant desideratum."[14]

Through a careful selection of bishops, Rome endeavored to consolidate its influence.[15] Preference for this office was given to priests who had studied in Rome. During the long pontificate of *Pius IX* (1846-78), theological "triumphalism" was fully victorious. The critical impulses of German theology were thoroughly suppressed. Until the 1950's it was scarcely possible to obtain information about these currents in Catholic theological faculties.

5. A new version of medieval scholasticism, the "ancient and pure teaching," took the place of this critical theology, a version completely lacking in a sense of history. This new scholasticism was effectively propagated in particular by the Jesuit theologians of the Papal Gregorian University and other papal colleges in Rome. The best known of these men were *Passaglia, Franzelin,* and *Schrader.* In Germany, *J.*

Kleutgen and *M. J. Scheeben* adopted this scholastic thought and developed it most impressively.[16] This "new" theology was approved for the first time by official curial statements in 1857.[17]

Neo-scholasticism was interested in the contemporary sciences only from an apologetic point of view. In substance it returned to a pre-critical philosophy and metaphysics. Its arid academic approach attempted to reproduce the philosophical and theological thought of an era long passed, in particular, the thinking of *Thomas Aquinas,* but without the slightest feeling for the intellectual originality of the true scholastics. Historical research was frowned upon. While the history of dogma was cultivated intensively, by and large both the Bible and the history of dogma were understood in an uncritical fashion as forerunners of the final formulation of dogmas.

Such a theology had the effect of producing a ghetto, since it effectively cut its students off from the movements of the time. As a result, it could flourish only where ecclesiastical control had produced the necessary social conditions, namely, in seminaries.

A man who himself played an active part during these times, *Ignaz von Döllinger,* called this new policy "the terrible system of repression in Church literature and doctrine." "The terrorism of the Inquisition throughout the Latin south," he continued, "and the Roman Index made impossible any spontaneous movement or self-generative progress in science and literature. The newly introduced practice of preventive (antecedent) censorship, unheard of in the Church before this time, required that every book be approved by three, four, or even five priest censors before its publication. These were almost always members of one of the large religious Orders. Each censor could strike out whatever he judged unsuitable. But he was responsible for what he let stand and would often be punished even by imprisonment for an unpopular passage

that had slipped his notice. This all seemed calculated radically to discourage all scholarly writing, where scholars were still
to be found. No grass grew beneath the brazen footfalls of
such institutions. Theology shriveled to the most indigent
form of scholasticism and stale casuistry. Biblical studies dis-
appeared. Historical research became simply too dangerous.
A historian could hardly avoid the suspicion of heterodoxy;
the very term *criticism* aroused mistrust and hate. . . . This
graveyard situation was then referred to as 'the consensus of
the Catholic Church in its virtual totality.' . . . Men who did
not belong to powerful religious institutions like the Jesuits
or Dominicans . . . could no longer be interested in writing
theology, so isolated and unprotected was their position."[18]

Only a monolithic Church, which had built a wall around
itself, so it was felt, could afford to disregard the attacks of a
hostile world. It was necessary to close ranks, theologically,
ecclesiastically, and politically, in order to be armed against
Protestantism, liberalism, atheism, nationalism, and soon, too,
against socialism.[19] National synods were forbidden.[20] The
spiritual ghetto was complete.

The Catholic Church historian, Rudolf Lill, writes about
this process: "The most negative consequence of this ultramontane concentration was the spiritual impoverishment
which the curia and its followers imposed upon the Church.
. . . Alongside the precipitous condemnation of new initiatives,
the retreat to apparently safe old positions had a second and
equally detrimental consequence. Rome lay a long way from
the centers of spiritual, political, and economic movements
in nineteenth-century Europe, and in Rome it was thought
possible to ignore the many developments in the natural and
social sciences."[21]

6. A number of critical theologians were condemned. Finally, in 1864, *Pius IX's* unsurpassed formulation of "triumphalist" theology, the *Syllabus of Errors,* was issued. It can
only be compared with the later anti-modernist theses of

Pius X. In primitive and generalized statements which avoided all substantial discussion, every contemporary movement was condemned: pantheism, naturalism, rationalism of every variety, indifferentism, Protestantism, modern theories about the state and society, critical ethical reflections, and, in particular, every new evaluation of marriage and sexuality. Condemned too was any discussion of even the *political* power of the Pope in the Papal States, attempts to obtain the right to free exercise of religion for Protestant citizens of Catholic governments, and so forth. There was even a movement formally to declare the *Syllabus* a dogma.

7. These currents could not have prevailed had they not been supported by strong religious sentiments. A triumphalist kind of piety led to a reanimation of parish life; priestly ordinations increased; religious Orders were founded for the care of the sick and for education, and laymen, too, became active in apostolic activities.[22] Cult and ritual also were practiced enthusiastically. "Pre-enlightened forms of piety" such as the veneration of the saints, pilgrimages, indulgences, and religious institutes celebrated a renaissance.[23]

The crowning example of this new piety was the proclamation in 1854 of the dogma of the Immaculate Conception of Mary. There was no theological need for this definition. "The doctrine of the Immaculate Conception had not been contested. The theologians who did not consider it a subject for definition, did not think it worthwhile to argue about it either."[24] The definition was not aimed at a matter of "doctrine," but at the object of this particular form of piety. At issue was a "devotional dogma,"[25] which made official a certain kind of Catholic sentiment.

Moreover, the Pope acted *alone* in proclaiming this dogma. Although he had requested the opinions of the bishops, no theological discussion took place, nor any form of consensus-building. "Thus papal infallibility was exercised in its most solemn form."[26] This anticipated in practice what Vatican Council I later defined in theory.

C. The Threat to the Papal States

The threat of losing the Papal States forced the Popes to counteract this deficit in political power with a surplus of ecclesiastical importance. As a result particularly of the Pope's being politically constrained, he gained in the eyes of the Catholic masses the aura of a martyr with whom one had to identify and show solidarity.

1.   The controversy concerning the Papal States had a strong influence on the decisions of Vatican I. These States had only been reconstituted in 1815 at the Congress of Vienna, and they were being governed in a shockingly authoritarian manner, in which spiritual sovereignty coincided with secular power. An authoritarian conception of the State was wedded to absolutistic conceptions of primacy, and thus ensued a total repression of the people. The Papal States were "notorious everywhere for their monsignorial mismanagement and social backwardness."[27]

Now the movement for Italian unification endangered the existence of these states and the papacy tried everything in its power to stem this development. The extensive expansion of the papal diplomatic corps in the 1850's doubtless was also intended to safeguard the Papal States. Nevertheless, they were doomed to disappear. In 1859/60 they had already been decisively reduced and only a French garrison prevented the Italian nationalists from taking the final step. With the outbreak of war betwen France and Germany in 1870, this garrison was withdrawn, Vatican I had to be recessed, and the nationalists occupied the city of Rome. Since that time only a few small properties remain "sovereign territory" and so maintain the fiction that the Vatican is a formal state.

2.   Under these circumstances, *Pius IX* felt compelled to counteract his political defeat by strengthening the position of the Church in other areas. While this was not his most

important motive for the convocation of the first Vatican Council, it surely played a part in his decision. Hans Küng describes the thinking of Vatican I as follows: "Almost the only ray of hope for those who, relying on Matthew 16:18, wanted at all costs to hold on to temporal power was the idea that no one would dare to take action against a Pope whose infallibility had been solemnly proclaimed *urbi et orbi* in an ecumenical council."[28]

3. Infallibility, according to Küng, would never have been defined were it not for the figure of *Pius IX,* who was initially "hailed as a liberal and a reformer," but "grew more and more reactionary, both in politics and in theology." He "also obstructed the Italian national unity movement with his consistently maintained *non possumus,* accompanied by continually reiterated emotional protests."[29]

Because of his popular manner and his sense of humor, Pius IX was widely loved. Soon he appeared as a defenseless victim of political machinations and a martyr of power politics. Precisely for this reason, the Catholic masses spontaneously identified themselves with him. "The common people found in the suffering Pope abandoned by the politicians an appropriate object upon which to focus their sense of fairness and justice—something for which the effort seemed worthwhile."[30] As Küng says, "the dogmatic tie that bound Catholics to the Pope was thus charged with feeling, and a completely new phenomenon appeared in the form of emotional 'veneration of the pope.' "[31]

It would seem, therefore, that the possibility of defining this dogma of papal primacy and infallibility in 1870 rested largely on this wave of ultramontane emotion "varying from extravagant declarations of loyalty to the Pope to blasphemous identifications of the Pope with Christ."[32] But resistance was not lacking. Liberal Catholics in France grouped around the periodical *Corespondant* and the Theology Faculty of the Sorbonne. Many professors in Germany in the 1860's, es-

pecially Ignaz von Döllinger, tried to promote a more discrimi-
nating and rational kind of thinking. But the process could
not longer be halted. Critical thinking had lost its bases in
the life of the common faithful.[33]

D. The Convocation of Vatican I

*The council was convened for a negative purpose: to
ward off the hostile forces of the spirit of the times. In addition, as a result of the development just described, the question of hierarchy and authority had moved to the center of
Catholic attention. The historical dynamic which inevitably led
to the definition of the primacy and the "infallibility" of the
Pope is comprehensible only in the light of these facts.*
1.   On December 6, 1864, two days before the publication of
the *Syllabus, Pius IX* informed the Cardinals of the Con-
gregation of Rites that he intended to hold an ecumenical
council in order "to remedy in this extraordinary way [by
means of a council] the extraordinary afflictions of the
Church."[34] Thus the council had a defensive character from
the very beginning; it was a question of building protective
dikes against the currents of the times. In addition, it was an
attempt to compensate for the imminent loss of the Papal
States by means of a council in which the Church would rally
round the Pope.

A secret polling of the Cardinals indicated that a strong
majority was in favor of the council. In an extensive document the German Curial Cardinal Reisach explained the need
for the council: the last council—the Council of Trent in
the sixteenth century—had not rejected clearly enough the
basic error (!) of the reformers, namely, "the denial of the
hierarchical structure of the Church and its infallible teaching authority."[35] Thus the process of political and ecclesiastical centralization had transferred the question of hierarchy,
primacy, and authority into the center of the Church's reflection. This context alone enables us to apreciate how such

basically peripheral, organizational questions became charged with so much emotional intensity.

A commission of Cardinals met for the first time on March 9, 1865, to begin preparations for the council. A partial poll of thirty-six bishops indicated that more or less all of them favored a clear delineation of Church authority. However, only eight bishops (!) advocated a definition of "infallibility." Nonetheless, it still took "two years before the Pope had overcome all his reservations"[36] and definitely made up his mind to convoke the council. In order to make this decision, he had also to overcome the reluctance of his Cardinal Secretary of State in particular, since the latter feared political complications.

On June 26, 1867, when nearly five hundred bishops were in Rome for the centenary of the martyrdom of Peter and Paul, it was solemnly announced that the council would be convened in order that "the necessary antidotes might be found for the so numerous evils oppressing the Church."[37] A year later, the opening date for the council was set for December 8, 1869, the Feast of the Immaculate Conception of Mary! All Catholic bishops and the Superiors General of the religious Orders were summoned. The bishops of the Eastern churches were also invited, but the Patriarch of Constantinople returned the invitation unopened because the Pope was lacking in "respect for apostolic equality and brotherhood."[38] Finally, on September 13, 1868, the Pope published a letter to Protestants and non-Catholics "in which he appealed to them to return to the fold of Christ."[39]

Although at all ecumenical councils up to this time, except for the Fifth Lateran Council, the participants themselves had determined the order of business, it was now specified by Rome. Five commissions, divided according to topical themes, were set up to prepare for the council. Their members were one and all representatives of Roman theology. Only at the insistence of several bishops were a few representatives of other schools admitted.

2. In the semi-monthly Jesuit periodical *Civiltà Cattolica* of February 6, 1869, a lengthy article signed by its "Paris correspondent" appeared. It demanded the definition of the theses advocated in the *Syllabus* as well as of papal "infallibility." These definitions, it was stated, should take place, not through discussion and voting, but by means of acclamation. The "article burst like a bomb."[40] Then Ignaz von Döllinger published his newspaper articles in the *Augsburger Allgemeine Zeitung;* in June of the same year they appeared in book form under the pseudonym "Janus."[41]

The Minister President of Bavaria warned against the consequences of such a definition, and the chairman of the Sorbonne, Maret, dissociated himself from the Jesuit article. Hubert Jedin writes that Maret advocated "a moderate Gallican conception of the Church. . . . Not papacy *or* episcopacy, but papacy *and* episcopacy together are the subjects of infallibility."[42] Under the chairmanship of the Archbishop of Cologne, Melcher, the majority of German bishops regarded the definition of infallibility as "less opportune." In a pastoral letter, they sought to quiet public opinion in Germany: "The council will not define any new or other fundamental tenets than those which through faith and conscience are written in all your hearts."[43] But the criteria for censure were again strengthened, and broad theological discussion became impossible.

E. *The Progress of the Council*

In spite of the resistance of an appreciable minority, Vatican I defined the Pope's full and direct primacy of jurisdiction over the whole Church and his "infallibility." The definition was not properly discussed from the theological point of view. Thus it was primarily a result of the current veneration of the Pope on the part of the majority of the Council Fathers.

1. The opening of Vatican I took place on December 8, 1869, with the largest number of participants for any council up to that time. "Of approximately 1,050 Catholic bishops, 774 participated."[44] A first-draft proposal, *Concerning the Catholic Faith,* "inspired by the *Syllabus,*"[45] was sharply criticized by the bishops. Yet, after many alterations, it was finally accepted in April, 1870. Representatives of the "Infallibilists"—advocates of defining papal infallibility—were active during these debates, and they succeeded in filling the pertinent commission with their own partisans. As early as December, 1869, 380 bishops had petitioned the Pope for this definition, although a document opposing definition had succeeded in obtaining 140 signatures.

Thus, at the beginning of 1870, two factions opposed each other.[46] The "Infallibilists" further managed to obtain an alteration of the procedural rules by which oral debate was restricted to a minimum. In the meantime, public discussion continued with undiminished vehemence. Ignaz von Döllinger declared: "From the beginning of the Church until today no one has believed in the infallibility of the Pope."[47] The attitude of heads of state was negative, but expectant. The Papal Secretary of State was so troubled that in March, 1870, he advised the Pope to withdraw the proposal, but without success.

2. The proposal in question bore the title *The Church of Christ.* It had been distributed to the Council Fathers in January. Ten chapters dealt with the Church in general, two chapters (11 and 12) with the primacy, and the remaining three chapters with the relationship of Church and State. Not until March 6, at the urging of the "Infallibilists," was a passage concerning papal infallibility inserted into chapter 11.[48]

Chapters 11 and 12 were expanded, divided into four separate chapters, and submitted to the plenary session on May 9. During the debate thirty-nine interventions were made *in favor* of the definition of infallibility and twenty-six *opposed* to it. Another forty still wanted to speak. At that point a resolution to end the debate was proposed by 150 bishops. "Against the protests of the minority,"[49] the resolution was accepted. The minority could still submit reservations about the text of the definition, but fundamental objections could no longer be raised.

3. The debate about the juridical primacy was relatively unproblematic. Chapters 1 and 2, dealing with the institution of the primacy by Jesus Christ and with the continuation of this office in the Church, were scarcely contested, since it was thought that Mt. 16: 1-19 and Jn. 21: 15 covered these matters. Problems arose only with Chapter 3, concerning the rights of the Pope—the unlimited primacy of jurisdiction. Nevertheless, here, too, the formulation stating the "full power to tend, to rule, and to administer the whole Church"[50] was finally accepted.

4. The voting on the draft proposal concerning papal infallibility took place on July 13, 1870. Four hundred fifty-one Fathers voted yes; 88, no; and 62, yes on condition that certain alterations be made. Because of this latter group, minor changes were included in the text. Then, in the final voting on July 16, the text was accepted almost unanimously, because most of its opponents had left the Council and gone home.

The whole Constitution, *Pastor aeternus,* was solemnly approved, with two negative votes, on July 18. Because of the beginning of the French-German War, the Council was recessed. Rome was taken by Italian troops on September 21. The end of the Papal States and the end of the secular sovereignty of the Pope had come.

5. Throughout the world, the Catholic population tumultuously celebrated the Council's decress. Serious difficulties arose only in Germany, but the German bishops insisted on obedience. "When Archbishop Scherr of Munich returned

from the council he said to Döllinger at his reception at the train station: 'Let's go to work!' To which Döllinger replied: "For the old Church!' The archbishop countered, 'There is only one Church.' Döllinger responded: 'They have created a new one.' "[51]

In August, 1870, Döllinger convoked an assembly in Nuremberg which questioned the freedom and the validity of the Council's decisions. In April, 1871, he was excommunicated. His followers founded the Old Catholic Church and, in 1873, established their own episcopacy.

6. Döllinger's objection about the lack of freedom of the Council Fathers was, however, only partly justified. As far as the majority of the participants were concerned, there can be no question of any direct suppression of freedom. But Döllinger was right if freedom is taken to mean not merely freedom of speech but also the possibility of broad-scale theological discussion and the dissemination of information. Still it would be better to speak with Hans Küng of the "ideological blinkers"[52] restricting the vision of Vatican I, since the possibility of such discussion did not exist. "Even after the announcement of Vatican I, theological discussion was not free of the fetters imposed on it by the curia of Pius IX. . . . As a result the advocates of other opinions were frequently forced to publish their views in the liberal press." Writings demanding a decentralization of Church government were put on the Index.[53] In this way, definitions which had not received adequate theological motivation came into being. Cardinal J. H. Newman complained to his bishop: "When has definition of doctrine *de fide* been a luxury of devotion and not a stern painful necessity?"[54]

PART TWO

Theological Analysis

In the following chapters we shall attempt, as succinctly as possible, to interpret the statements of Vatican I against the background of their history. Chapter 8 presents more general conclusions, while chapters 9 and 10 propose a more positive understanding of "primacy" and "infallibility," with a view toward ecumenical possibilities.

Chapter Eight

The History of Primacy: The Teaching of Vatican I

A. History as a Criterion of Interpretation

The definitions of Vatican 1 concerning the primacy and the infallibility of the Roman bishop are (provisionally) the final results of a long history. Consequently, one cannot adequately reflect on these definitions and interpret them without taking this history into consideration. Any interpretation which takes as its point of departure the ahistorical wording of the conciliar decrees—and nothing else—misses the essence of the matter. To proceed in this fashion is to interpret not the dogma but ourselves; it is to seek a plausible explanation of our short-lived tradition with the help of the dogmatic formulation. But this is useless in an area in which the questions of papal primacy and infallibility are at issue, since these can be understood only in terms of their history.

B. The Meaning of Appeal to the New Testament

The study of the history of the Roman primacy has shown that Catholics must resign themselves to the fact that the New Testament does not support claims for Peter's position of primacy, nor for succession to that position, nor for papal infallibility. What we are speaking about here is not a politically motivated position of priority for a big city community, but the *theological* appeal to Peter's primacy to justify that of the bishop of Rome. It is only this latter which constitutes the beginning of the *theological* history of the primacy. As our study has shown, it is now clear that this theological appeal to Peter's primacy first appeared only relatively late in the history of the Church. As far as the history of ideas is concerned, the way to this theological claim was prepared for by a juridical understanding of the New Testament statements about Peter. But it was not until perhaps Stephan I in the third century, and certainly Damasus I toward the end of the fourth century, that these passages were first used in theological argumentation. In the subsequent period, this mode of argumentation gradually gained acceptance in the Western Church and thus provided the foundation for the statements of Vatican I.

Consequently, no historical foundation exists in the New Testament to justify the papal primacy. The concept of this primacy is, rather, a theological justification of a factual situation which had come about earlier and for other reasons. It is a *theoretical superstructure* erected upon current or past developments. This is not to deny that the concept of papal primacy made history in its own right once it had been postulated.

This observation is really not so startling when we consider that many Christian phenomena have developed in the same fashion. Various official Church structures have simply arisen in the course of history; only after they had come into existence were attempts made to justify them theologically. The doctrine of the sacraments, for example, was in the process of development up until the twelfth century. Other examples are the teaching about the institution of the sacraments by Christ, the biblical canon and its theological justification, clerical celibacy, and all the efforts to find exegetical foundation for it.

The process of *post factum* theological certification of actual developments can be found throughout the history of the Church. Often it has produced contradictory results; or rather, it was often used to justify historical phenomena in a way which a consensus *today* recognizes as being incorrect.

The theological justification of the medieval feudal system or the modern class system, the Christian certification of kingship and monarchy ("by the grace of God"), the anti-social or anti-emancipation measures following upon the theological justification of striving for law and order, are all examples of this process. Yet nobody, not even a conservative Catholic, continues to take such theological justifications seriously once the phenomena which motivated them have become historically obsolescent. Today, for example, nobody gets excited when the biblical justification of the secular sovereignty of the Pope or the medieval prohibition against taking interest on money is said to be unfounded.

But what is valid for historical processes that are past and done with cannot be excluded *a priori* from applying to other processes which are still historically significant. This conclusion cannot be avoided with respect to the theological justification of papal primacy. It has developed historically *and* it is still relevant for a part of Christendom. Yet basing it on the New Testament amounts to a post-factum theological superstructure. This statement sounds negative, though it is painfully inescapable. It does have an undeniably negative aspect. Theological justifications can often serve to congeal processes which had better been left fluid. As a result of the appeals to Scripture made by Vatican I, the state of development of papal primacy achieved in the nineteenth century has been considered sacrosanct and untouchable ever since. But the historical-critical perspective compels us to "demythologize" and ignore this taboo.

Nevertheless, we should not overlook the fact that this conclusion does not constitute an absolute verdict with respect to using Scripture in this way. Up until now there has been practically no reflection within theology about the very fundamental difference between historical-critical exegesis on the one hand, and the application of Scripture in "Church" usage and in official Church documents on the other hand.

From the point of view of historical-critical exegesis, for example, almost all the biblical citations used in dogmatic hand-books to justify various dogmas are used incorrectly. Almost all the biblical passages in Council decrees, even those of Vatican II, are cited without regard for their original context. It would be easy to demonstrate this assertion.

One conclusion is forced upon us by this observation. Unless we are willing simply to dismiss as "uncritical" the ordinary Church usage of the Bible, we must keep in mind that the critical and the "Church" usages belong to separate and distinct existential situations (*Sitz-im-Leben*), and each of them seeks to express something different. Exegesis intends a critical analysis of the textual material and its content. The "Church" usage of Scripture, on the other hand, is not primarily concerned with the text at all. The center of attention here is rather the desire to show that some contemporary concern (a dogmatic statement, a Church structure, a political decision) is both *legitimate for the Christian* and based *upon Christian inspiration* in the Gospel. Support for the prohibition of usury by citations from the Bible, for example, can only mean that obeying the prohibition is considered to be a Christian duty. The biblical passages cited may actually have had nothing at all to do with the matter at hand.

The correctness of this statement can easily be verified on the basis of the whole of Church history. Wherever a certain way of acting, a historical development, or a conviction was deemed legitimate and right, it was understood as *Christian* duty. This peculiar kind of necessity is characteristic in the history of religions; similar phenomena are found outside Christianity too. Since the origins of Christianity are found in the Gospel as recorded in Holy Scripture, this Christian legitimacy was necessarily articulated *in the words of Scripture*. The Old Testament is already cited in the New Testament in the same manner. In the process, considerable liberties were taken; all the biblical passages which seemed in some way to fit the context were cited by *association*.

The purpose of this *associative argumentation* in the Church's usage of Scripture is to exhibit the Christian legitimacy of one's own convictions—nothing more. Consequently, this usage should make no claim about the *historical-critical* legitimacy of such Scriptural quotations. Thus it should be clear that this usage of Scripture is not really "false" just because it is unsound in terms of the criteria of historical criticism.

We would misunderstand the argument of Vatican I in using the New Testament passages concerning Peter if we sought to deduce from them the contention that the Council teaches that Peter is in effect the first Pope, even in some incipient fashion. Unfortunately some highly uncritical Catholic dogma studies still do just this. In spite of contrary appearances, such an exegetical assertion was not intended by the Council. Rather, in citing these biblical passages the participants in the Council wished to profess their conviction that the historical development of the primacy of the Pope, which they accepted, expressed a Christian truth. Better still, it represents *the* Catholic verity. They considered papal primacy, as it had developed, to be a historical consequence of the Christian mission.

Assertions which go beyond this view only misconstrue its existential situation, its *Sitz-im-Leben*. The task of contemporary Catholic theology, therefore, cannot be to provide an exegetical justification for papal primacy as such. It must rather ask itself to what extent and within which limits the content of the assertion intended by the Council in its own time continues to be valid today: that papal primacy is legitimately Christian.

There is no argument against the facts, but the review of its history has shown that the possibilities open to Catholic theology faced with the dogma of 1870 are greater than, up to the present, they have been considered to be. Catholic

theology is free to view papal primacy as a phenomenon arising in post-biblical times; it is free to view the "biblical"
foundation of this phenomenon as an ambivalent assertion:
positive in its intention (the primacy is legitimately Christian), but possibly negative in its effects, since this primacy
cannot be discussed because it is considered sacrosanct.

In addition, Catholic theology should examine the extent
to which the definitions concerning primacy and infallibility
have the character of dogma. For it is also Catholic conviction that dogma must have biblical foundations or, rather,
foundations in the Gospel. And, of course, this foundation
must now be shown in terms of the textual evidence ascer-
tainable via historical criticism. It was, after all, the same
Vatican I—probably without being aware of the significance
of its statement—which asserted with respect to papal infallibility: "The Holy Spirit was *not* promised to Peter and
his successors in order that they might promulgate through
his revelation *a new doctrine,* but that under his guidance
they might preserve and faithfully interpret the revelation
transmitted through the apostles, or the deposit of faith (*depositum fidei*)."[1] The faith transmitted through the apostles,
i.e., in Holy Scripture, may not be expanded by new teachings.
Every interpretation must be proved to be the interpretation
of apostolic doctrine.

C. Succession in the Primacy

Our historical study has shown that the *theological* history
of papal primacy begins only in the third or fourth century.
Before this time the "priority" of Rome developed gradually
on the basis of its political position and, in the West, of its
(double) apostolicity. Further, it would seem that, in all
probability, the Roman community existed for several genera-
tions—until about 130 A.D.—without a monarchical episcopacy. Yet the primacy defined at Vatican I pertains to a
bishop and not to a community.

It follows, then, that there can be no question of the "un-broken succession" (succession in office) of the Roman bishops to the "primacy of Peter." As history shows, a certain importance of the Roman community and its bishops developed first; justifying this importance by asserting that the bishop of Rome was the successor to Peter's primacy came later.

In view of these facts, the dogmatic conviction of Catholics concerning an unbroken succession of Popes from Peter is untenable if understood as a historical judgment about what actually took place. Still, it need not be "false" in every sense. In much the same way as the appeal to Holy Scripture, it has other than historical value. It gives expression to the Christian *profession of faith,* the understanding that everything Catholics are as Christians derives from Jesus Christ and from His mission. To say that "the Church possesses an unbroken succession from the apostles" means that what constitutes the Church as such is not derived from itself, but is given in and with its origins.

Thus, in relation to this profession of faith, it is perhaps correct and comprehensible that the Church should regard all its "truths" as forming an unbroken sequence, even though this may not be historically demonstrable—whether these be concerned with Church office and ministry, the faith, or papal primacy. Since such argumentation is not intended to include historical description, there would be no contradiction if, for example, one of the Lutheran National Churches were to maintain that it, too, is grounded in the apostolic succession. Although both statements would be historically inaccurate, the profession formulated in both the Catholic primacy and the Lutheran ministerial structure are the same: our present Church structure is legitimately Christian. Which profession is *substantially* more correct cannot be decided by historical research, since other criteria are valid here. Therefore, in Church or confessional language, the biblical and the historical type of argument represent *different kinds of speak-*

ing. In other words, the research methods of form criticism current in exegesis must also be applied to the history of dogma. This is a hermeneutical necessity.

D. *The Acceptance by the Church of the Claim to Primacy*

The *claim* to a position of primacy made on behalf of the Roman bishops and the *recognition* of this theory by the Church are two different matters. A long time passed before the Roman demands were accepted as valid even by a portion of the Church.

The *Eastern Church,* which after all comprised the majority of Christians until its decimation by the Islamic conquests, never recognized a Roman primacy of jurisdiction. At most, a certain priority of honor was conceded to the bishop of Rome on occasion, and usually with reluctance.

In the *Western Church,* the Roman community was increasingly able to enhance its prestige. As time progressed, the Roman bishops also became increasingly stronger in jurisdictional matters beyond the borders of their own region. Yet these activtities do not seem to have exceeded the capacities appropriate for the central and apostolic city of the West. The claim to primacy in Rome was only made with any continuity after the end of the fourth century. It is safe to assume that recognition of the theological justification of these Roman initiatives only occurred in these other communities from that time on.

Even then, the Roman claim remained for the most part a theoretical matter for long periods of history until the eleventh century when, as a result of all sorts of developments, it gained great practical importance following the "Gregorian reform." Nonetheless the Roman claim was not seriously contested in the West after the end of antiquity, though this was chiefly due to its limited practical relevance. Finally, since the Reformation, the papal claim to primacy is no longer recognized in a large part of the Western Church either.

The conclusion to be drawn from these observations is that Roman primacy was never a structural element of the order or constitution of *the* Church. In the light of its history, the primacy must be seen as a central element of the constitution of *one* of the Christian Churches. Measured, for example, against the equally "late" development of the monarchial episcopacy at the end of the first century, the organizational model of papal primacy appeared only very late in the Western portion of the Church; it took hold very gradually, and definitively only since the eleventh century. Soon afterwards, however, with the Reformation, other models of Church organization replaced it in a portion of the Church. Since then, papal primacy is a structural element solely in the ecclesial organization of the Roman Catholic confession.

Catholic theology was able to demand that all churches incorporate the Roman primacy into their own ecclesial organizations as a condition for the unity of the churches only so long as the Catholic Church understood itself, as it once did, to be the sole legitimate form of Christianity. But at least since Vatican II, this can no longer be maintained. *On the other hand,* this demand was only possible because the horizon of the participants at Vatican I was limited to the Western Church, with the behavior of the Reformation churches understood only as a "falling away" from the true path.

For a more global view of history and for a new theology which sees the ambivalent—positive *and* negative—possibilities in all basic forms of church organization, this demand is unrealizable. No form of church organization was ever valid universally. All forms have their own history and all are more or less "ancient." Although the episcopal is an older form, the institution of the patriarchate is at least no younger than that of papal primacy. Similarly, all forms of Church organization can give more or less sound theological grounds for their existence.

Consequently, since the primatial model of organizing the Church is supported neither by the New Testament nor by unbroken succession, nor by a general or even a widespread acceptance, a very radical question must be raised. Did the participants at Vatican I intend to define the Catholic form of Church organization as *the only legitimately Christian one,* and even as the only possible one for the future? *Or* did they want to profess *for themselves and their situation* that they viewed the primacy of the Pope as an optimal and central structural element of the Church? Are the definitions of this Council simply dogmatic statutes, or are there theological reasons and criteria for these theses?

E. Development in the Content of the Idea of Primacy

With regret Joseph Ratzinger observes "that a widespread lack of clarity has existed in history about the precise nature of the office of primacy."[2] A statement like this is possible only for someone who stands at the provisional conclusion of a historical development and, with at least an approximate conception of the nature of primacy, tries to discern its historical origins.

Ratzinger says that the Council of 1870, while still leaving single questions open, nonetheless brought about a fundamental clarification. In view of this achievement, Ratzinger deems it possible to define the primacy more precisely. It is not a mere priority of honor. "Neither does its nature necessarily include Rome's position as administrative center (centralism), but only the spiritual-juridical fulness of responsibility for the [preaching of the] Word and for the *communio* (the community)."[3] Ratzinger finds that the misunderstanding of papal primacy as administrative power is based on the fact that the *primacy over the whole Church* and the *patriarchal power over the West* have become so intermingled in Western thinking that they can hardly be distinguished any more.[4] Therefore, he is convinced that the idea of primacy would be unaffected by "a far-reaching patriarchal 'autonomy'" (for example, in the event of a reunion with the Eastern Churches).[5]

At first glance, this theoretical distinction in the actual exercise of the power of primacy between a spiritual-juridical responsibility (belonging to its nature or essence) and an administrative central power (not belonging to its essence) seems very plausible. But examined more carefully, it looks much less convincing. What is a "spiritual-juridical fulness of power" without any "administrative competence" whatsoever? What should the Pope's primacy of jurisdiction still consist of if it is only "spiritual-juridical"? Can the Pope still act effectively in the Church? If need be, can he depose a "heretical" bishop or annul the decrees of a synod? If so, how does this differ from central administrative power? If not, just what constitutes the content and extent of his jurisdiction? *Juridically,* one can only distinguish greater and lesser administrative power, or the claim to fulness of power and its perhaps less comprehensive actualization. Thus Ratzinger's distinction does not seem to lead any further; it is only a verbal solution to the problem. It is probably intended to be a help in apologetics. Against attacks on Roman centralism, one can then concede generously that the central administrative apparatus really has no value. It doesn't belong to the essence of the primacy and can perhaps, we may hope, be someday modified.

In addition, Ratzinger's historical knowledge surely forced him to make this distinction. He tries to take historical reality into account when he observes, for example, "that the full-fledged medieval idea and actualization of the primacy may not simply be superimposed on the more restricted forms of earlier times."[6] Christian antiquity knew no primacy of administrative jurisdiction, though it did recognize certain powers of the Western patriarchate.

But precisely here we must reject the tendency of Ratzinger's exposition. His distinction clearly serves to justify the decisions of Vatican I concerning papal primacy, at least its "spiritual-juridical" scope. But history shows all too clearly that a jurisdictional primacy in any way resembling the definition of 1870 only began to take effect after the "Gregorian reform." Ratzinger uses history in an apologetic-dogmatic sense. Unfortunately he neglects to show where this distinction was ever made in history. In addition, he seems to misconstrue the real context. *Rome's spiritual-juridical claim is the result of its actual ("administrative") competence, and wherever it has been made, the dynamic of this claim was always directed toward its actual validity,* that is, toward administrative power.

From the discrepancy between papal claims and their actual realization in pre-medieval times—in effect, up until the eleventh century—one may not conclude that the Popes of that time made a spiritual-juridical claim which allowed the continued existence of the administrative autonomy of bishops or local national churches. It was not as if the Popes intervened only sporadically in virtue of their patriarchal powers. Rather, from the time when theological argumentation for papal primacy first began, the Popes had an eye also and especially toward the actual exercise of their power. At the time, however, they were unable to put this theory into practice. The increase of their power in the Middle Ages naturally tempted the Popes to make ever broader "administrative" demands. But this in no way proves that previously they had intended to restrict themselves to the role of a "spiritual-juridical" authority.

Furthermore, the extreme formulation of the "spiritual-juridical" competence of the Pope at Vatican I did not produce some "pure" and "trans-historical" dogma, which regrettably in the course of history had been and was distorted by elements foreign to it—such as a central administrtion. The examination of history rather forces on us another interpretation. In earlier times the theological claim to primacy was a "superstructure" erected upon an actual power position developed along the lines of the tradition of Roman hegemony. So, too, the extreme theological formulation of the universal and immediate papal primacy of jurisdiction can only be understood against the background of the Pope's administrative power position, which had escalated to extreme proportions in the nineteenth century. Never before had the Pope enjoyed such a position. The practice, reflection, and emotion of the Church was so strongly focused on the figure of the Pope because of the destruction of the self-assured national churches and the triumphalist tendencies of political, ecclesiastical, and theological currents, that the articulation of this dogma became possible and somehow even historically inevitable. The definition of 1870 can only be understood as the attempt to secure for the Pope immediate and universal *administrative* powers in the whole Church.

In the light of possible practical reforms, it may well serve a purpose to point out that even this administrative centralism can allow for a certain freedom of self-administration. To some extent such freedom has been allowed, as a gesture of good will, in the case of the Eastern Uniate Churches. But such tactical considerations cannot be made part of the interpretation of dogma, in order to reverse its historical, that is, its true inner structure. If one studies history to see how the content of the primacy claim has developed, it becomes evident how very intimately this feature has been related to the actual possibilities of exercising Roman power. In their actual content, the claims to papal primacy prove to be a function of the actual administrative position of the Roman bishop extended in the line of the tradition of imperial hegemony. Both this factual position and, as a result, the "definition" of its content have been subject to constant change.

What, for example, would a dogma concerning papal primacy look like had it been defined in the fourth, the seventh, or the thirteenth century? *There is no Church reality corresponding to the dogma of 1870 in the third, seventh, or tenth century!* Transplanted back into those times, it would stand in a vacuum.

Thus it is difficult for theologians in any way to demonstrate the "dogmatic" character of the 1870 definition. Is this dogma at all a matter of the definition of Christian truth, *or* is it only a formulation in theological terms of the actual state of the papacy's ecclesiastical influence in the year 1870? Much can be said for the fact that the more detailed conciliar statements concerning the primacy of jurisdiction should not by considered dogma binding the Church for all time. The definition apears to express the intensity of feeling within the Catholic Church seeking to close ranks around the Pope and to declare that this situation was legitimately Christian. The intent of the definition seems to put walls around the actual state of canon law and current Catholic practice in order to defend them against attack.

The question is whether a conciliar decision previously understood as a dogma is still today a genuine ("spiritual-juridical") dogma, or only the description and formulation of an actual administrative situation that cannot be rejected *a priori* as "un-Catholic." A passage from the 1969 "Declaration of the German Bishops concerning the Priestly Office" will help clarify this matter. This declaration states that the Reformers' challenge to the specific office of the priesthood forced the Catholic Church to formulate its own understanding at the Council of Trent. "In point of fact, the definitive form of the Council's decree only considers the questions of transmitted 'Catholic doctrine' contested by the Reformers. Thus the dogma it proclaimed represents a clarifying justification of the *actual* office exercised in the Church rather than a comprehensive theological reflection on the problems at hand."[7]

This statement more or less clearly concedes that the dogma in question, in opposition to the Reformers' practice, "rather" expresses the Catholic mode of Church structure and confirms that it is Catholic. But can the expression and justification of a specific legal practice be an "irreformable" dogma in the strict sense? Can juridical norms or even structural matters ever be established in a fashion valid for all times?

The central administrative position of the Pope has become even stronger between Vatican I and Vatican II. New technical possibilities for rapid and uninterrupted communication have made absolute centralization for the first time fully possible. Increasingly throughout this period the reality of the Church has coincided with the dogma of 1870.

More recently, however, the position of Catholics in Western democratic societies has led to a sense of the inappropriateness of this absolutist system in the Church. Vatican II reevaluated the office of bishops and granted that they, too, have responsibility for the administration of the universal Church. In establishing the Roman Synod of Bishops, Paul VI began to implement this concept—even though the Synod is not functioning properly yet. More and more church groups and even whole regions feel that *their* mode of Christianity requires a new Church structure, one which no longer coincides with the nineteenth-century mode expressed in the dogma of 1870.

Because of the 1870 dogma, the demand for a change in Church structure in the light of new social realities will initially seem to be heterodox today, even though in the past the Church has changed in this way many times. But the reproach of heterodoxy can only be seen as a political move in the context of mere organizational matters. Similar phenomena can be observed in reproaches of heterodoxy leveled against opponents of the sovereignty of the Pope over nations at the time of Boniface VIII, for example, or against opponents of the theological justification of the Papal States before Vatican I. That a specific matter is thought to be a *question of faith* at a certain time is not an absolute guarantee that it actually corresponds to the *depositum fidei*. At very least, such a conviction cannot provide an *a priori* criterion which cannot itself be called in to question by virtue of the reality at issue. If it could, theology would have to abandon its claim to be a critical science. It would become merely a methodically exact and systematic presentation of Christianity in the light of the dominant Catholic world view at the time.

F. The Doctrinal Competence of the Pope as a Function of His Juridical Power

History makes it clear that the concept of the competence of the Pope in matters of doctrine has roughly corresponded to the current state of development in the concept of papal primacy. When, for example, in late Christian antiquity the Roman bishop possessed a certain prestige, his legates at ecumenical councils used this to advantage, even though the papal opinions they advocated were nothing more than the views of a very important bishop. Much the same can be said for other interventions of the Pope in matters of doctrine. His jurisdictional and "magisterial" capacities were already greater in the West; they became even more comprehensive in the Middle Ages, notwithstanding long periods of stagnation.

Nevertheless, these phenomena should not be overrated and interpreted in the sense of the later dogma. Until the ninth century, even in Rome the synodal form was considered to be the ordinary and binding form of magisterial activity. "In order to emphasize the regularity and canonicity of decrees, the papal legates, and even the Pope himself, occasionally point to the synodal form of decision-making. At the time of the Fourth Council of Constantinople (869), regular and synodal, is a stereotyped formula. One has the impression that only synodal decision-making is considered regular. Even Pope Hadrian II used this formula in his letter of June 10, 869, to Ignatius."[8]

Ever since the fourth century, the Popes sought to gain

influence at synods. "Resistance to papal claims can be observed in East and West."[9] De Vries asks, "To what extent
have these claims been made effective?" He points out that
"in his Constitution *Immensa* (January 22, 1588), Sixtus V
still had to affirm and enjoin that decrees of provincial synods
be submitted to the approval of the Holy See."[10] Some synods
and councils did apply for this approval, but others sharply
rejected the claim. "Nonetheless, a *struggle* can be observed
between a conception of primacy advocated by Rome and
tending toward *absolutism,* and a *collegial* understanding...
which prevailed at the councils."[11] Thus, what is at issue
here is not the question of truth itself, but a struggle over
juridical competence.

The conviction in the Western Church that it is heretical
not to be in union with Rome has only come about since the
"Gregorian reform" when the papacy set itself up as the
actual leader of the whole Church. But it was the Reformation more than anything else that forced the Catholic Church
to make the papacy the center of its attention. As churches
became divided on the basis of different "confessions" of the
faith, the Pope and the question of truth were fused. The
most important steps, with respect to the history of ideas,
toward the extreme formulation of the Pope's magisterial
competency at a later date occurred at that time, although the
later conclusion was not then drawn. On the contrary, the
thesis of papal infallibility which arose occasionally since the
thirteenth century was intended to bind the Pope to the decrees of his predecessors; it sought to restrict his magisterial
authority, and this is why the thesis was forbidden at the papal
court.

The most important step, however, was taken in the
Counter-Reformation. Still, for such an extreme thesis of
infallibility to become effective in practice, an actual primacy
was also needed, such as developed in the nineteenth century
in the form of an absolutist monarchy. Only then, and against

resistance, did the formulation of the Pope's absolute doctrinal authority become historically feasible, an "infallibility" which was the noetic counterpart of his absolute administrative authority.

Yet even Vatican I set limits to this infallibility. Thus, although the Pope is not required to obtain the consent of the "churches," but can proclaim dogmas *ex sese,* nevertheless he can only exercise his infallibility when and because he speaks *ex cathedra*—in a most solemn and highly official form—*as* Shepherd and Teacher of all the faithful. According to the words of the Council, only then does he possess that infallibility which Christ intended for the Church (as a whole).

This makes it clear that the Pope is "infallible" *as* representative of the Church for whom he speaks. He participates in the *Church's* infallibility. Because this Council viewed the person of the Pope as the incorporation of the Catholic Church, it conceded to him, when speaking *ex cathedra for this Church* in matters of faith and morals, that power which it claims for the Church as a whole, that is to say, "infallibility," whatever is understood to be the content of this concept.[12]

The absolutist fulness of power in governing the *Church* is something which concerns the preaching of the Gospel, the *true* Gospel. From the inner logic of the matter this must also include a definitive doctrinal competence. But this amounts to nothing more than what was granted very much earlier to ecumenical councils. Because they represented the whole episcopacy and thus, according to the opinion of the time, the Church, their definitions concerning faith and morals were considered to be true, inspired, and irreformable—in a word, the qualities intended in and by the later concept *infallible*.[13] The same conclusion necessarily led to the teaching concerning the "infallibility" of the Roman bishop wherever he represents the Church. Consequently, the "triumphalist" Council confessed that it encountered the truth of the

Gospel "infallibly" in the Church which exists under the Pope's central leadership.

Therefore, the 1870 definition of papal infallibility does not regulate a "purely" doctrinal mater, a question of faith and morals, in distinction to the juridical definition of primacy. Rather, infallibility stands and falls with the absolutist primatial constitution of the Church. This too is in the final analysis a *juridical* matter, a question of Church order: *how and in which institutions* does the Church give expression to itself and its conviction of faith? The theologian, too, in his interpretation of this "dogma" is faced with the difficult task of demonstrating to what extent a "dogmatic" character pertains to this element of Church order arising under the conditions of the nineteenth century.

The relationship between absolutist primacy and "infallibility" is also apparent in the fact that the latter has been exercised only twice in the sense of the Council's definition: once by anticipation (1854) in the proclamation of the dogma of the Immaculate Conception of Mary, and then (1950) in the proclamation of the dogma of the Bodily Assumption of Mary into Heaven. Both times it was a matter of "devotional dogmas." Both occurred in periods of triumphalist thinking—1950 falls within the period following World War II. Both were proclaimed by extremely autocratic Popes, Pius IX and Pius XII. Yet not even these two Popes neglected the opinions of the bishops, but asked for their votes prior to promulgating the definitions. Thus, the *ex sese* has yet to be exercised in a very extreme manner.

When, in a new period of history, modifications and changes are made in the Church structure which has existed since the eighteenth century, a logical consequence of the process will be to raise once again the juridical question of the institutional representation of the Church in matters of truth, that is to say, the question of (papal) infallibility. When Vatican II revalued the role of the episcopacy in the government of the universal Church, a minor correction was already made. Nothing forbids or makes heterodox the assumption that in a future Church society the concept of an absolutist competence in government and truth will seem increasingly problematic. As the ecclesiastical and theological situation becomes ever more differentiated and complicated, the carrying out of the tasks of leadership *and* doctrinal competence will no longer be possible according to the monarchical nineteenth-century model. Indeed, one can hold the opinion that, while the definition of infallibility in 1870 appropriately expressed the experience of the majority of Council participants at that time—i.e., that it is "true"—it has no meaning for the future, because it no longer serves a purpose.

Chapter Nine

The Theological Relevance
of the 1870 Definition of Primacy

A. *Papal Primacy as an Element of a Particular Church Structure*

Papal primacy refers to an "office in the structure of the Church's organization."[1] More precisely, it refers to an office of the Catholic Church's structure. Examination of the history of papal primacy forces us to recognize that it is *not,* as Joseph Ratzinger presumes, founded "on apostolic tradition and in the final analysis on a commission which comes from the Lord."[2] It does not even go back to the oldest layer of Church history, nor was it ever accepted generally as *the* structural form of the Church. Thus we see how very acute is the problem of the theological legitimacy or even necessity of precisely *this* Church model in comparison with the structural modes of other Christian Churches.

No Church structure can lay concrete claim to be derived from Jesus of Nazareth, nor even in any conclusive way to derivation from the New Testament. The post-Easter mission apparently began without any organizational model at all. At the time, no one ever gave a great deal of thought to such matters, since the expectation of Christ's imminent return made them seem superfluous. Because the circle of Jesus' disciples, and especially the Twelve, alone could guarantee continuity, they naturally enjoyed a special position. Beyond that, anyone who felt called to do so exercised certain duties and services, and many offices soon arose in the Church, as one can learn from the Epistles of Paul. The office of *community leadership* exercised by a number of

"elders" became more important only as community relationships started to be established. The establishment of stable
community structures was made necessary by the new situation in which the early communities had to prepare for an
indefinitely prolonged future. The figure of the individual
"bishop" first emerged out of the circle of presbyters toward
the end of the first century. The formation of a monarchical
episcopacy occurred gradually and was completed by the third
century.[3]

Thus the Christian communities themselves created Church
structures which were in some ways quite diverse. Their development in New Testament times and afterwards makes
it impossible to assume their institution by Jesus or even to
claim for them "apostolic" institution. The incipient organizational models were clearly conditioned by the historical
situation of the Church at the time, and new situations demanded new models in order that the Gospel be proclaimed
effectively. Each Church structure was intended to help
meet contingencies in a *practical way*. The motivation for
the development of new forms of Church order, and like-
wise their criterion, was clearly *pastoral-theological efficiency*.

Pastoral-theological efficiency seems to be the sole specific,
positive *theological* criterion for each Church structure.[4] As
a guiding principle in all further processes of development, it
can be observed throughout Church history. Apart from the
new beginnings of a few "reform" movements,[5] however,
the weight of structures established in the past has often been
so great that processes of change initially appear only as further
developments or changes of existing forms. Notwithstanding
their conservation of traditional structures, however, these
changes not infrequently led to qualitatively new Church
offices—for example, the "president" of the primitive Christian community developed into the sacerdotal priest.

On the basis of any other criterion than that of pastoral-
theological efficiency, it does not seem possible to justify the

primacy of the Roman bishop as an element in the structure of a particular Church. The historical development of this structural element shows how the Roman bishops, in the interest of Church effectiveness, expanded their field of activity everywhere they could, up to and including the extreme "Catholic" position at the time of Vatican I.

Like every (non-Reformation) Church structure, that of papal primacy was not developed on the basis of abstract reflection: how can the preaching of the Gospel be accomplished optimally today? Rather, this practical theological criterion was the motivation for *further development and change in already existing structural forms. Here, the particular relevance of the City of Rome and its inherited claim to worldwide hegemony already existed. This tradition cannot be underestimated. A Christian community in the capital city of the empire had already existed, which could soon lay uncontested claim to its foundation by Peter and Paul; besides, it was a community enjoying prestige in the West precisely because it was the sole apostolic commuity there. And preexistent also was the North African juridical exegesis of the New Testament passages concerning Peter in favor of the office of bishop.*

It is thoroughly understandable that processes of change growing out of practical necessities fastened upon these preexistent historical forms. In retrospect, this development even seems almost inevitable. The comprehensive Church activities made necessary by the "Constantinian turning-point," the political and ecclesiastical vacuum of power in the West in late antiquity, the new tasks arising from the appearance of the Germanic tribes, the universalist trends in the High Middle Ages: all these new social, ecclesial, and theological situations constituted so many *challenges* which led to corresponding Church structures. In view of preexistent contingencies, nothing was more likely than that Rome respond to these extensive tasks by developing extensive new organizational forms, with Rome as the center. Notwithstanding continuity with established structures, in successive new phases of a long process, structures that were thoroughly new (with respect to their theological quality) came into being.

As it was finally defined in an extreme form in 1870, the primacy of the Pope thus appears as a concrete Church structure resulting from and in continuity with preexistent historical structures. The occasion for papal primacy and its justification are found in the criterion of the most effective realization of the Church that was possible at the time. The form of papal primacy which appeared at each stage along the way was contingent on many historical factors: the character of certain historical personages, the favor or disfavor of the hour, excessive papal claims as well as the proper fulfillment of duties, guilt and sanctity, and so on. Like every history, the history of the primacy is ambivalent. The structure of papal primacy which emerged from this history shares with every other possible structure the ambivalence of promise and rigidity, efficiency and obstruction of possibilities. Still, a crystallization of the structure formulated in 1870 and articulated in concrete legislation in the Code of Canon Law in 1918, if permanently fossilized, would be completely contrary to its own history up to this time, and could no longer do justice to the pastoral-theological criterion which must remain an enduring postulate.

B. The Pastoral Theological Function of Papal Primacy

Rome's claim and its activity always possessed a certain trans-regional dimension, the dynamic of which soon reached out to the universal Church. This was true irrespective of which phases of development (since the third or fourth century) are under consideration, and irrespective of what theological and historical arguments were employed to substantiate the claim of the Roman bishops. It is true that Rome's claim beyond the borders of its own territory corresponded to the actual reality only to a very modest extent for long periods of time. Nevertheless, part of Roman reality has always been its consciousness of responsibility toward the "universal Church."

In this respect, the Roman bishops performed a truly *important service in bringing about communication with the universal Church.* For the Church in the West, Rome was the binding link to the East. Through Rome, the Eastern churches were informed about the thinking in the West. Rome's function of communication was even more important within the Western churches. Many threads came together in Rome; it was the best place to discover what a synod in Spain or France had decreed.

For the young German local churches in the beginning of the Middle Ages, Rome performed an indispensable function. On the one hand, it was the only way to transmit to them the inheritance of the ancient Church and the Patristic Age. On the other hand, it was the only way to prevent an ecclesiastical "Balkanization" of the West. Similarly, had it not been for the papacy, more universal Church structures would never have come about in the High Middle Ages.

Corresponding to Rome's *activity* in the universal Church, there was also a certain *expectation* on the part of the individual churches. Communion with the Roman bishop was felt to be a genuinely positive element of belonging to the Church. By and large, this communion with Rome consisted in fact in a predominantly passive agreement in principle together with occasional communication. After the Gregorian reform, however, these forms of communication and unity finally became more concrete and binding. By the nineteenth century, they achieved their most extreme expression in the model of absolutist primacy and corresponding obedience— though this was still only valid for the Catholic Church.

The specific theological character of papal primacy thus consists in its ability to make Church unity and comprehensive communication structurally possible. Although the concrete forms of unity and the binding force of her mechanisms have been very different in the course of history, at all stages of development the primacy of the Roman bishop has constituted an *office of unity.*

Unlike other elements of Church constitution such as the diaconate, priesthood, and episcopacy, this office of unity was not incorporated into the sacramental doctrine of the Church, for the simple reason that the theology of the sacraments had acquired its definitive form, at the latest, in the twelfth century. This form still prevails within Catholic areas of the Church. At the time of the formulation of sacramental doctrine, however, consciousness of the relevance of this office of unity was still too new, and later there was too much reluctance to break up the closed sacramental system. Nevertheless, this reluctance did not prevent the "non-sacramental" primacy from impinging upon the autonomous significance of the other "sacramental" stages of Orders: deacon, priest, bishop. Not until Vatican II were certain modifications made for the office of bishop, but these have yet to take effect in any real way. If anything, the dependence of bishops upon the Pope has even grown since the Council.

C. *The Theological Significance of the Office of Unity*

The unity of the Church is constituted in very diverse and manifold ways. Even for Catholic teaching, as Karl Rahner says, the papacy is not at all "the sole principle of unity in the Church. The unity of the Church derives first and foremost from the Spirit of God and it is given to the Church and preserved (by the Spirit).... With respect to the visibility of the Church, the Eucharist, too, is a principle of unity in the Church. In the realm of faith, the one Scripture has a function ... constitutive of unity."[6]

Rahner's list is certainly not taxative, but it suffices to show that Church unity is more than a point of reference in

Church structure. Even the factors just mentioned as constitutive of unity are more than just "spiritual" elements.
The *one* faith and the *one* hope, the *one* Lord Jesus and the
one Scripture also have a historical dimension. Thus, even
if there were no primacy, Church unity would not be trans-
ported into a supra-historical, "invisible" realm. Of all the
possible historical-spiritual factors of unity, papal primacy
is one which has emerged from a specific *Church structure.*
It is the official-organizational, institutional expression of and
effort toward Church unity—a unity which is also manifest
in other ways.

What might be the significance of such an ecclesiastical
office of unity? It is sometimes maintained that, since so
many different church structures have existed throughout
Christian history, an office of unity is incompatible with the
nature of the Church. On the structural level, it would be
sufficient for Church unity if the churches could reach a common understanding among themselves as sister communities
within the one Church, and if they would recognize and toler-
ate one another without making dogmatic claims to ex-
clusiveness. This argument cites the long periods in the early
history of the Church when no more institutional unity than
this existed.

Nevertheless, this idea amounts to a theory justifying the
status quo. One can understand, of course, why it has reap-
peared, since the current practice of Roman primacy in the
Catholic Church seems to allow no greater accommodation
to other churches than a shoulder-shrugging toleration at most.
But we should not overlook the fact that a false practice still
does not eliminate the theological meaningfulness of a unity
that is *also* expressed in institutions. *Abusus non tollit usum*
(misuse is no argument against right use): this too is a
fundamental Roman principle.

History at least refutes the idea that churches can exist for
long without unifying institutions. Incipient unifying elements

are to be found even in the earliest phases of the Church, when communities were fully absorbed in internal matters and in missionary activity to the surrounding world. Confessional formulas were distributed among different regions; Christians were received into foreign communities as brothers in faith; and a modest exchange of information took place.

With the success of missionary activity in the Mediterranean world, the Church was forced to develop comprehensive unifying "institutions." It was necessary for local churches to work together in tandem with a unified State institution and in the propagation of theological currents of thought throughout the Empire. The first synods met and, with the "Constantinian turning-point," the era of ecumenical councils began. Parallel with these developments, transregional structures came into existence, ranging from dioceses to patriarchates.

Thus, as soon as the energies of ecclesiastical life were no longer utilized on comparatively insignificant matters of local concern, theological and other movements impinged upon these boundaries, common political tasks arose, and the Church began to develop institutional forms; and this made action possible. Since some problems affected numerous communities, they had to be solved in common; and it was necessary to establish communion with one another to initiate dialogue and to strive for a binding consensus—all of which made institutions necessary.

Even the churches which emerged from the Reformation could not and can not get by without institutionalized forms of unity. Although by virtue of their theological tradition they tend to be very reserved with respect to church structure, they do establish national and regional churches, and meet at national convocations of both a confessional and inter-confessional nature. Even at the worldwide level, there are confessional (e.g., the International Federation of Lutheran, or Methodist, Churches) and inter-confessional (e.g., the World

Council of Churches) institutions.

It does not seem possible to get along without institutionalized unifying structures. Theologically, they can be seen as
social and "political" consequences of the fundamental Christian unity, the unity of faith and of preaching the Gospel.
An ecclesiological dualism which makes a radical distinction
between the one "invisible Church" and a pluriform "visible
Church" split into many factions is, in the final analysis, un-
Christian. It is true that the full (redeemed) unity of the
churches, and of mankind, is an eschatological achievement,
a component of the Christian hope for a better future with
God. Nonetheless, this faith must be realized within history
and must produce ever new attempts at communication and
at least a minimum of unity even amid great diversity.

Solidarity and unity among persons are not static realities
but tasks which must be constantly worked out anew. For this
reason, the churches need to develop certain mechanisms and
"institutions" in order to facilitate communication between
the most diverse groups; *de facto,* they have always done
this. If the desire for unity is to be more than merely verbal,
there is a need for institutionalized communication mechanisms and communication centers.[7]

What form these institutions take is theologically indif-
ferent:

—a tacit agreement within the Church to come together in
  general council in cases of severe conflict, such as was the
  practice for a number of centuries;

—such meetings agreed to on a cyclical basis;

—bodies created to meet on a regular basis while maintaining
  offices in the interim (e.g., the World Council of Churches) ;

—a single bishop, as would be natural for an episcopalist
  church structure, facilitating communication (in this case,
  the bishop of Rome, since history pleads for it) ;

—some mixed form, as was long the Catholic practice: the
  bishop of Rome took over the "day-to-day business" of pre-

serving communication, while synods were convened for regional or difficult inter-regional problems.

Such an institutional form for facilitating a "universal" Church community through communication and the mutual resolution of conflict is only meaningful, however, if it is feasible and efficient at a particular time—the pastoral-theological criterion. This means, *on the one hand,* that there is no form which can be valid for all times. Even if it were desirable that the bishop of Rome be the center of Church communication forever, the concrete form of primacy would constantly have to change. This process of change is documented in history. Papal primacy can only continue to exist if it moves on from the form most recently defined in the nineteenth century. *On the other hand,* the requirement of effectiveness for a unifying institution demands that it restrict itself to a minimum of basic activities. Only in this way can it be acceptable as a partner in dialogue for a multitude of churches and groups; only in this way can it effect communication and bring divergent views to some acceptable compromises.

Although there have been genuine failures, by and large in the course of its history the Roman episcopate has performed this indispensable task of constant renewal with basic self-restraint. For long periods of time, Rome alone fostered mutual information among the churches. The most important unity-creating function of the papacy for the greater part of its history consisted in the convocation and leadership of general councils which facilitated discussion among divergent groups. In matters of theological controversy, Rome often exhibited an exemplary restraint that achieved much in the service of unity. A classical example is the controversy concerning grace (about 1600) in which the Jesuits and the Dominicans were both tempted to accuse each other of heresy. Pope Paul V made *no* decision and condemned no one. Thus he avoided a fateful division and could regroup the opposing parties around Rome as their center.

But such specific theological activities of the "office of unity" as have been customary since the begining of the nineteenth century will contribute inevitably to the division of the Church. Since Vatican II, such actions have attained a new intensity. When the papacy abandons its necessary self-restraint in an attempt to establish a particular current of thought—e.g., Roman theology—at the expense of compromise between *all* other trends, the office of unity is perverted into a source of discord. If the World Council of Churches were, for example, to try to force Lutheran or Eastern Orthodox theology upon all its member churches, its end would be near. Its institutionalized effectiveness for the achievement of unity consists precisely in its fundamental decisions concerning a very few propositions acceptable to all parties. On this basis, it facilitates dialogue among groups which hold different views. It is self-restraint, primarily, which enables the office of unity to become a *service* to the Church. Otherwise a destructive *domination* emerges.

To an office of unity facilitating actual communication necessarily corresponds a *commitment to communion* on the part of the churches: acceptance of the actions of an "office of unity" which is effective, and is recognized for that reason, cannot be simply optional. This office must possess *juridical* or *jurisdictional* competence. An institutionalized *mechanism* of unity can function only if it can claim the right to make some kind of binding decisions with respect to the continuation of communion and the initiation of dialogue—only of course on the basis of a minimum of common Christianity shared by all parties. *Vice versa*, the single churches must have a certain *juridical* commitment not to abandon unity, but to remain in dialogue.

The clearest and "most perfect" unity is uniformity. Precisely with respect to unity, a Church that is a monolithic block with identical world-wide structures, theologies, and practices may seem to be the ideal solution. The thinking of Vatican I was certainly not devoid of such a concept. But monolithic orthodoxy and uniformity in a society can be attained only by means of an absolutist and totalitarian central government. For that reason, the nostalgia for "orthodoxy" in nineteenth-century Catholicism necessarily generates the formation of a consistent, more or less absolutist conception of papal primacy coupled with administrative centralism.

But such uniformity can only be maintained for short periods of time. Otherwise it necessarily brings about the separation of whole groups from the Church and the inner or outer emigration of many individual believers. In the long run, central administration cannot prevent a plurality of ecclesiastical and theological forms. An office of unity that sought such uniformity would be doomed to failure. Total central administration does not create unity; what does is the complying with the principle of subsidiarity. "For the Pope (and even more for his administrators) there exists . . . a sort of *principle of subsidiarity*. That is to say, the Roman functionaries should not take upon themselves tasks that the bishop and his diocese can manage."[8] But acting in accordance with this principle cannot mean an office of unity which is "in itself" universal, possesses immediate jurisdictional competence, "concedes" areas of autonomous self-administration. Subsidiarity is rather one of the juridical components of unity.

D. Concrete Forms of the Office of Unity

After all that has been said, it can no longer be maintained theologically that the Roman primacy is the only Christian form possible for the office of unity. The primacy of the Roman bishops is rather *that* form—fundamentally plausible from a theological viewpoint—which has developed out of historical contingencies. Papal primacy is one form of the office of unity that has emerged alongside others (e.g., episcopal, synodal, or patriarchal) and which has also proved itself effective in the course of history. It arose on the foundation of imperial Roman tradition and the establishment of a monarchical, episcopal Church structure, with unity perceived as personified in individual figures. Through a combination of both these elements and justified by "associative" theological argumentation, the current form of primacy is the result of a forceful concatenation of circumstances and the bold initiatives of many Roman bishops. This stage of development fixed in the nineteenth century has proved to be *one* concrete form alongside numerous others in the past. Nor will it be the last form. Vatican II has already made certain reforms in a feudal episcopalist nature. The fact that these reforms are modeled on past forms of Church structure should not be overlooked. They are atavistic modifications, but for that very reason they can be easily justified: "it *was* this way before." It is as if the papal primacy developed on the model of absolutism were to be modified by recourse to still older models of constitutional monarchy or feudalism. What is needed, however, is the development of *new* forms that incorporate the much lauded "emancipation of the laity." The laity are no longer satisfied simply to delegate their responsibility to the bishops. There is need to establish *democratic forms*.

From a theological point of view, the concrete forms of the institutions of unity are provisional. They need not stand in the way of a new ecumenism encompassing all churches. But it would be utopian to think that the search for new forms could start all over again from the beginning. As always in the past, so too in the future the weight of established structures will continue to be felt. New models are only possible when conventional forms are modified and further developed, although in time this process can produce *qualitatively* new forms. Future institutions of unity will have to emerge on the foundation of conventional structures.

As was previously noted, non-Catholic churches also have their unifying institutions. Heading the list is the World

Council of Churches. It is perhaps not completely utopian to seek to combine both forms in the future—the World Council and the Roman primacy. The time for the Catholic Church to join the World Council of Churches is overdue. After this step, a new form might arise by way of compromise, a World Council of Churches in which the Bishop of Rome, while renouncing all exercise of sovereignty, could act as president. However, before that can happen—if it ever does—many things still have to change within the Catholic Church. First, new forms both of the appearance and the exercise of papal primacy must be developed which correspond to the new situations in the Church.

E. A Theological Evaluation of the 1870 Dogma of Primacy

For the definition of papal primacy, as for every dogma, it is not the literal text of individual assertions that is "dogmatized" and hence "irreformable," but the content of the dogma, the substance of which is justified by the New Testament confession of faith.

For the evaluation of the statements of Vatican I concerning papal primacy, the following conclusions seem to emerge from our study.

1. The *theological* assertion of the definition could be formulated:

a. The Catholic Church adheres to the belief that unity among Christians is an eschatological hope, the impulse for which comes from Jesus. However, in its following of Jesus, the Church must strive after this hope symbolically, historically, concretely, and in a minimal, but basic way.

b. The Catholic Church is convinced that this Christian unity must be sought ever anew and that it needs historical institutions and mechanisms in order to make unity "politically" feasible.

2. In addition, the Catholic Church in the nineteenth century professed *for itself* that it sees a concrete realization

of the office of unity in the historically venerable institution of the Roman primacy. (It realizes that it is not speaking for all Christians in this matter.) Notwithstanding contradictory statements from non-Catholic sources, the Catholic Church holds that this concrete form is legitimately Christian. (This statement is founded on the New Testament and in history in an "associative" manner.)

3. In addition to this, the Catholic Church at that time, thinking in a contemporary idiom, professed its belief in the juridical absolutist stage of development of papal primacy as it then existed.

Thus, the aspect stated under *1* can be qualified theologically as "dogmatic" in the technical sense. The statement in *2* is the expression of that positive relationship to one's own tradition that must be accepted in any social body which does not wish to lose its identity. Point *3* represents a legal development specific to a certain period of history.

Chapter Ten

The Theological Relevance
of the 1870 Definition of Infallibility

A. The Office of Unity and Doctrinal Competence

We have already seen how the concept of the doctrinal competence of the Roman bishops grew gradually stronger in the course of history. This concept, we said, is the noetic or gnoseological counterpart of papal primacy. In other words, a Church that is committed to preaching the Gospel *truth,* and thus is constituted on the question of truth, must also and necessarily develop its administrative competence in the realm of preaching.

Preaching, too, takes on an "official" character in the Church wherever certain bodies or institutions express and represent the unity of regions and groups in the Church, and particularly when they represent the "universal" Church.[1] A pastor "responsible" for a community speaks more "officially" than just any member of his community. According to traditional theology, a bishop has teaching competence for his own diocese, a bishops' conference for the region it represents, and a Council and/or the Pope for the whole Catholic Church.

In principle, Vatican I did nothing particularly exceptional when it attributed a definitive competence in doctrinal matters to the Pope. In effect, it simply drew the final conclusion from a principle that had always been operative in the Church. This could happen because "previously" the office of unity—the primacy—had been raised to the height of its jurisdictional position.

However, the linguistic usage of the 1870 definition is reductive in this respect. Every institution of Church unity is concerned with the question of truth. There can be no logical separation of jurisdiction and "magisterium" in the Church. But this correlation does not mean that increased administrative power makes preaching any more "true." It simply becomes *more "official."* What the pastor says is not any "truer" than the word of some member of his parish, but only more official. So, too, the bishop speaks more officially than a pastor, but not necessarily any more "truly." By the same token, ultimate "truth" does not immediately pertain to an administrative primacy of the Pope conceived in an absolute way. What the Pope says only possesses an ultimate "officialness" for the interpretation of the Gospel at any given time.

The cumulative official character that pertains to a doctrinal definition formulated by this office of unity cannot simply be identified with "infallibility" in teaching. First of all, this official character only refers to the *canonical* (from Canon Law) requirement that all communities "subject" to this office—rather, those who acknowledge it—accept such a definition as "true" or "false." An "office of unity" can speak officially for the Church to the extent that it is accepted. It binds the Church *in law* to official promulgations.

This statement might have sufficed for Vatican I. In that case, it would, in a logically precise fashion, have extended the *juridical* character of the papal primacy of jurisdiction to cover the juridical aspect of representation with respect to doctrine which belongs to this primacy. But in defining the *"infallibility"* of the Pope, the Council went a step further. The definition was possible only because the Council shared the traditional conception that the Church as a whole is "infallible." For this reason, the official representative of the Church also participates in its "infallibility." The majority of the participants at the Council wanted to bind the Catholic Church *in law* to the official definitions of the Pope. But this immediately posed a problem. How can a Church be "infallible" if its entire preaching is based on official statements that might be "false"? In light of the whole tradition, the only response the Council could give to this question is that such dualism is impossible. Consequently, the *ex cathedra* definitions of the Pope are "infallible."

Theologically, therefore, "infallibility" and an "office of unity" for the universal Church do not immediately belong together. The character of office is first of all concerned with officialness. The question of "infallibility" belongs *in another context,* namely, whether it is legitimate to understand Jesus' promise of the Holy Spirit for the Church in the sense of an "infallibility." And, secondly, is the Church still "led by the Spirit" when it adopts official Church doctrinal statements that are possibly "false"? It is at least open to discussion whether the Council's definition clearly envisaged these two questions and, consequently, whether they received a *binding* answer in the definition. There is reason to believe that the Council did not take a clear stand on these issues. Without actually reflecting thematically on them or professing them, it seems that the Council simply adopted the traditional theological opinion that official promulgation correlates with truth, as well as the traditional conceptual usage of "infallible" with respect to Christian truth. This thesis is further supported by the fact that the Council wanted to clarify the position of the Pope and was not concerned with the theological problem as to whether a distinction exists between universal Church "officialness" and truth.

Precisely *this* question would have needed to be discussed for a *theological, dogmatically binding* definition. The discussion could not have been restricted to the "officialness" belonging to the Pope, for this is only *one* specific institutional instance of universal Church obligation. Lack of such theological discussion at the Council indicates that *its sole concern was the juridical question of the binding power of papal doctrinal statements within the Church.*

We would not claim that the problem of "infallibility" was not even raised in connection with the "dogma" of 1870. We only wish to clarify what was the concern at that time and, consequently, what was defined in 1870. There is only a *heuristic* relationship between the *papal* role and the question of the "truth"—or, as it was expressed in rationalistic terminology, the "infallibility"—of the binding force of dogmatic formulations by the papacy for the universal Church in questions of faith and morals. The more fundamental problem was not raised in 1870, but was thought to have been clearly "solved" in the sense of convictions handed on from ancient times. In other words, the Council did not formulate the binding force of *ex cathedra* papal definitions in the linguistic categories that pertain immediately to the matter itself. Without further reflection, it used traditional concepts that only indirectly—in a second stage—relate to the actual question.

B. The Pastoral Theological Function of the Pope's Universal Magisterium in the Catholic Church

The possibility granted the Pope by Vatican I to speak officially, and thus with juridical binding force, for the whole Catholic Church in matters of doctrine does not derive either from the New Testament or from ancient tradition. Thus the question of the theological legitimacy of such an authority arises here too. We have seen that teaching authority is a component part of papal primacy. Like this primacy, so too the Pope's universal magisterium in the Catholic Church is justified *only* by *practical theological* considerations.

At all stages of its development, the function of the papal "office of unity" is the historical realization of communication and communion, and Christian teaching is an essential aspect of this function. From the end of antiquity until well into the Middle Ages, the papacy was a center of information and publication. It thus prevented the complete disruption of Church theology and language. The theological and linguistic split between East and West could not be avoided. But the Church's success in the West was due not least of all to Roman mediation, so that in spite of much diversity the Church nevertheless preserved at least some common fundamental points of "doctrine." Communion with Rome and occasional exchange of information was maintained at least passively. This helped to prevent the churches from allowing the Christian faith to be completely dissolved into popular traditions and cultures.

From the time of the "Gregorian reform," convictions in the universal Church were already expressed in a more juridically binding, more "official" form. The official function of the papacy with respect to doctrine was particularly strengthened by the Counter-Reformation. In the nineteenth century, finally, the official and unitive doctrinal role of the Pope could be formulated in an extremely absolutist sense.

At all stages of development, the official role of the papacy in doctrinal matters was founded upon its function in facilitating and—more or less by demanding it—effecting the historical institution of unity, even in preaching. The doctrinal primacy of the Pope is only legitimate because of its *pastoral theological* effectiveness in facilitating unity in faith and doctrine.

C. The Theological Meaning of Unity in Official Teaching

Once the attempt to work toward the unity of pluralistic churches is seen as a historical task, it becomes necessary to demonstrate this unity by documentation, with respect also to the most crucial question for the Church, namely, the preaching of the Gospel. As a result the Church has always seen doctrinal unity as guaranteed by several common and basic propositions. Concerning these matters, there has always been a more or less express agreement in spite of all existing plurality.

Notwithstanding a certain peripheral haziness about the

biblical canon, all churches accept in principle the Old and
New Testaments, for example, Confessional formulas and
liturgical texts have been received and handed down in the
"whole" Church—the so-called Apostles' Creed, for example,
has been widely disseminated as an official element of Church
language. Beginning even in New Testament times—the so-
called Apostolic Council in Jerusalem—attempts have been
made to settle through regional or general councils theological
controversies that threatened unity. Where the controversies
were less acute, communication in "normal" cases concerning
doctrinal matters was taken care of by bishops, metropolitans,
patriarchs, or, in the West, by the Roman bishop.

Of course, the more or less official binding force of the
elements, formulas, and institutions of "universal Church"
unity never produced a unity of doctrine and faith in the
Church in the sense of uniformity—although Vatican I apparently had such a guiding idea in mind. Plurality in theology and language has always existed. But, for a number of
centuries at least, total disparity and with it the breaking up
of the Church was prevented. Acceptance of the official elements of unity made it possible for all the various churches
to speak to one another on the basis of a language "all" accepted. After times of vehement controversy, for example,
when the contesting parties had agreed at a general council
on a common linguistic arrangement, plurality itself was in
no way eliminated. But the formula of union provided once
again a basis for linguistic and theological communication.

Whether formulas of union are informal like the "Apostles'
Creed" (i.e., not formally decreed), or emerge from synodal
agreement or even through the agency of a single figure of
unity like a metropolitan, patriarch, or Pope, they can have
juridical binding force in the Church only when they effect
minimal and fundamental compromises among the divergent
groups. Any further attempt to articulate a specific theology
or to help one church group to victory would only destroy the

chances of these "uinons" being accepted as juridically binding. History provides examples here too.

What is valid in principle for the "offices of unity" applies as well to its "magisterial" element. *Only the basic self-restraint of this doctrinal institution can make its decisions part of the common official linguistic usage of the Church.* The necessary minimal character of doctrinal statements that possess effective binding force makes clear that they express the faith of the *Church.* Because of its plurality with respect to doctrine, the Church can only be defined in a basic way.

Theological discussion needs to start at this point concerning these fundamental formulas that are juridically binding in the "whole" Church. If the possibility is left open that they may not only be one-sided and fragmentary, but even actually distort the Gospel, then how can one still speak about the "truth" of the Church's preaching of the Gospel and its appeal to its hearers? This possibility constitutes such a total ecclesiological dualism that truth and unity would be transferred to a meta-historical realm; the concrete Church and the Gospel it (who else?) mediates would become completely arbitrary. Thus, even though the concept of "infallibility" is a rather inappropriate expression of what is meant by "Christian truth," it still formulates a not unessential aspect of official doctrinal competence. However, it is distorted by its connection with the purely juridical matter of the institution of primacy and, therefore, becomes a possible source of scandal.

D. Roman Doctrinal Primacy as a Historical Form of the Institution of Unity

A separate but no less interesting problem concerns the *practical-juridical mechanisms* or *stable institutions* by means of which the Church achieves unifying formulas in matters of faith and morals.

The papacy was never considered the only institution responsible in this area. Even *after* the 1870 definition, Catholic theology recognized that binding—"true"—Church doctrine can be found in the general consciousness of faith in the Church (however this is conceived), in the ordinary preaching of the Church (the *magisterium ordinarium*), and in definitions of ecumenical councils confirmed by the Pope.

The institutional mechanisms for achieving ecclesiastical-theological consensus have been subject to constant change in the history of the Church. In comparison to the long history of Christianity, the ultimate doctrinal competence of the Pope is a very recent development. Institutional forms are clearly conditioned by current circumstances in a given society. The Church must fulfill its task of preaching the Gospel in and under these contingencies. Thus we can understand once again why, under the presupposition of the nineteenth century, precisely *this* arrangement came about.

In today's world and Church, and still more in the future, no juridical form of doctrinal competence can be irrevocably normative. Protestant churches try in part to make their criterion the still barely developed "models" from "apostolic times." The Orthodox churches are oriented toward the four great councils of "classical times." For the past century the Catholic Church has based its claim on the legal definition of 1870. All the churches have developed their own forms, but none of them can continue to be effective in the future without changing. The ecumenical agreement all desire will certainly have to create new institutions. However, these will have to be based on the historical forms developed up to the present—anything else would be utopian. Nevertheless, we can be sure of one thing. The heyday of purely confessional unifying formulas and purely confessional unifying institutions is past, even though these continue to exist.

A new consciousness is beginning to be formed in the churches, the consciousness of a fundamental unity of faith among all Christians in spite of existing confessional and inner-confessional plurality. This new common Christian understanding will scarcely continue to acknowledge the binding force of definitions that carry a purely confessional stamp. This means that such definitions will no longer be accepted as fundamental expressions of the faith of *the* Church. The influence of this principle has been an object of experience for some time now. Thus, Catholic theology should ask itself more directly why certain "Catholic" doctrines are finding so little actual acceptance among Catholics: the Marian dogmas, the 1870 definitions, the assertion that only validly ordained priests can celebrate the Eucharist, and others as well. The same question applies to a number of distinctively Protestant teachings. On the other hand, the fundamental Christian tenets are acknowledged in fact in absolutely all confessions. This new consciousness will become even more marked in the future.

Vatican II already considered this tendency when it resolved to formulate its decrees with an eye to non-Catholic Christians, and to omit anything which might deepen the separation. This was a first step, but in no way sufficient. Genuinely effective, and consequently minimal, definitions can be reached only when the other groups also are actually involved in the decision-making process. In view of the complexities and the plurality of problems and tendencies, only synodal and "democratic" institutions can be effective. A monarchical and personally oriented institution of unity was historically effective at one time. In the future is would seem to be an impossible form. Traditionalist reform movements in the direction of a feudal or constitutional structure which allow the bishops participation in the *magisterium* are equally inadequate.

E. A Theological Evaluation of the 1870 Definition of Infallibility

From what has been said, the following conclusions seem

logical:

1. In the light of tradition, the Council is convinced that the truth of the Gospel can be found in the preaching of the Church.

2. The Council professes its belief in the need for juridically binding, official formulations of the faith of the "universal Church."

3. The conviction that universal Church formulas are "true" ("infallible"), while not the immediate object of "dogma," is nevertheless taken over from tradition and reaffirmed. The Council professes its belief that these formulas in truth accord with the Gospel of Jesus.

4. The Council professes its belief for the Catholic Church that the primatial structure represents a legitimate form of the institution of magisterial unity, both historically and theologically. It is aware that it does not speak for all Christians in this matter.

5. In accord with the triumphalist phase of Catholic Church history current at the time, the Council granted the Pope the power to promulgate binding dogma even without his actually obtaining the consent of the bishops.

Statements 1-3 are theologically relevant and can be considered dogmatic assertions—though they are not formulated here for the first time, nor are they immediately "dogmatized." Point 4 is a profession of the Christian legitimacy of a historically conditioned form of Catholic constitution. Point 5 concerns a more detailed canonical arrangement.

Concluding Remarks

If it has succeeded in showing nothing more than that the unity of the churches need not be a hopeless venture, the preceding study has achieved its goal. When certain kinds of Catholic argumentation and conceptual models are clothed with an aura of dogmatic untouchability and irreformability, then such a venture appears to be historically hopeless. Of course, there are similar difficulties in other churches, but the Catholic theologian must address himself primarily to his own tradition.

Study of the history of papal primacy should make clear that there are *no theological* grounds preventing the future development of new forms. From the theological point of view, all forms of ecclesial organization are capable of being changed. On the other hand, certain structural elements have such venerable age and historical importance behind them that they cannot be simply dismissed in a revolutionary fashion. The future will have to produce forms which, in an *evolutionary* way, *transcend and make for a higher unity than the pluralistic models of the past*. Such a process can only begin when intra-confessional theological reflection has cleared the way by removing theological taboos.

Numerous convictions thought to be inalienable elements of Christian faith in the course of history have later turned out to be historically conditioned and thoroughly "reformable." Had anyone asked a first-generation Christian whether the proximity of the second coming of Christ was part of the faith, he would doubtless have said yes. Today we view this conception differently. If one could ask a thirteenth-century Roman theologian whether it pertains to Christian faith that the Pope is superior to kings, he would surely agree. Today we have little use for such an opinion.

Or again, the participants at the Council of Trent believed in the transmission of original sin through the act of procreation. They also thought paradise to be an actual condition. Pius XII still held that monogenism—the origin of mankind from a single pair—is a constitutive element of Christian faith. The non-dogmatic character of such conceptions often becomes apparent only in retrospect. The same may someday be said of numerous other "dogmas"—the idea of Mary's biological virginity, her bodily assumption into heaven, etc. In all these instances, theology has moved and continues to move forward. Apparently it is not the depth of understanding of the people who formulate an assertion which is decisive as to its "dogmatic" character.

The participants at Vatican I would also have affirmed that the literal texts of their definitions possessed a binding dogmatic character. But this cannot "forbid" critical examination at some later date. Should it become evident that the precise content of these "dogmas" is really concerned with problems that are largely juridical and organizational, this could not be denied by referring to the understanding of the Council Fathers.

Juridical arrangements are not the object of faith. They belong to the practical "political" realm. The desire to fix them forever and declare them "irreformable" amounts to a divinization of history. When, in the sense of traditional theology and Vatican I, the term *divine right (ius divinum)* is used with respect to the primacy of the Pope, for example, we should be aware of the *metaphorical character* of such language. On the one hand, papal primacy has not been handed down from heaven, but has genuinely developed in the course of our human history. And, on the other hand, even the dogma of infallibility applies only to questions of faith and morals and not to questions of Church structure.

From the theological point of view, the path is open to developing new structures. Whether or not we decide to walk this path is a "political" decision—a political decision between ecclesiastical and confessional conservatism and a will to reform which is open to the future.

Postscript for the American edition
——The Lutheran-Catholic Dialogue in the U.S.A.

In the United States since 1965, a mixed commission of the Lutheran Church and the Catholic Church has been studying the possibilities of rapprochement. It has attempted to delineate the differences separating the two. The work of this commission is particularly important because its twenty-six members were appointed by the governing bodies of the two Churches. Thus the results of its work have a more "official" character than the private research of individual theologians. However, it remains to be seen whether the Churches will acknowledge the results of this study.

The commission first examined interpretations of the Nicene Creed, baptism, the celebration of the Eucharist, and Church structure in general. The discussion indicated significant possibilities for mutual understanding. Finally, since 1971 the commission has turned to the question of papal primacy, the most difficult matter separating these Churches.

Four publications have emerged from this last phase of the commission's work:

1. The report of a subcommission in a book about *Peter in the New Testament*. This report examines the relevant New Testament passages and interprets them in a critical but unpolemical light. The Catholic editors concede that the New Testament offers no positive grounds for a primatial office of leadership by a single Christian. The Lutheran theologians express willingness to acknowledge that the later development in the ancient Church toward a position of Roman priority need not contradict the New Testament, and that it can even be seen as guided by the Spirit.

2. On March 4, 1974, a 5,000-word joint declaration was issued in Washington, D.C., bearing the title, "Ministry and the Church Universal: Differing Attitudes toward Papal Primacy" (*Origins*, N.C. Documentary Service, Vol. 3, No. 38, March 14, 1974). Both parties are convinced that any actualization of a new church unity will still require a long time. Nevertheless, priority is given to the need for a form of unity that is not only "spiritual," but also has a historical manifestation. This is declared to correspond to the will of Christ. It is even conceded that an individual office-holder (such as the bishop of Rome) *could* assume this responsibility.

However, no consensus could be reached concerning possible *forms* for a primatially structured unity. The models from the Church's past are felt to be insufficient. At best, a still inaccessible future might contain forms in which the Pope could "exercise his office in a manner better suited to the universal and regional needs of the Church under the complex circumstances of our time."

Thus the main problem seems to be the matter of papal jurisdiction. In addition to recognizing the positive function of the Popes for the *Catholic* Church, the Lutheran theologians could well imagine a reformed model of the papacy as the sign of pastoral unity. However, any exercise of jurisdiction beyond this they consider to be a restriction of the freedom of the Gospel.

3. In separate papers (together about 7,000 words) both parties once again spelled out their positions in detail.

a. In spite of bad examples to the contrary, the Lutheran theologians expressed appreciation for the papacy's frequent positive initiatives in the service of effective communication and unity in the Church. But they see no concrete possibility of acknowledging the primacy, and hope for future reforms.

b. The Catholic commentary begins with the fact that a simple integration of the Lutheran Churches is impossible. However, it maintains its own intention more concretely than does the Lutheran position, and proposes the elaboration of a "particular canonical status." This status must make it possible for the Lutheran Churches to acknowledge the primacy without forcing them to give up their own structural forms and adopt "all" (!) the current juridical claims of the papacy.

Such interconfessional contacts are always welcome—see, too, the conversations between Anglican and Catholic theologians. For Catholics, they help dissolve a historical positivism that sees in the actual course of history the unquestioned work of the Spirit. For Protestants, they help dismantle a distrust of concrete forms of historical unity—a distrust well-founded in the past and, unfortunately, in the present as well.

In addition, the theological contents emerging from the American commission's study are considerable. However, the great breakthrough has not succeeded, because these discussions still had to be carried on under the hard "Catholic *a priori*." The Catholic partner could concede that contemporary forms of primacy, including the methods used in the practice of papal doctrinal competence, are historically conditioned and genuinely reformable. Indeed they need reform, perhaps even to the point where the Pope would refrain from exercising his jurisdiction over some member churches. Nevertheless, the Catholic partner still had to maintain the "divine right" of primacy and the dogmatic quality of papal "infallibility."

The intention of my own study was to examine the legitimacy of precisely this "Catholic *a priori*," in order to facilitate for Catholics a genuinely unbiased ecumenical dialogue. The concrete juridical features of a future institution of unity can only be open to ecumenical discussion when it becomes clear that both the primacy of an individual Christian—the bishop of Rome—and the teaching concerning his "infallibility"—are the results of many circumstances in a *juridical* history and not "dogmas" in the proper sense.

Fortunately, the Lutheran participants in the above commission granted that Church unity should be manifested in a concrete and visible way. Thus they discarded a latent ecclesiological dualism existing in Protestant circles which makes a radical distinction between the *one* "spiritual" Church and its many divergent historical forms. Still, the insistence of the Catholic theologians (for which they cannot be blamed personally) on the jurisdiction and doctrinal competence of an *individual* office-holder prevented them from going a step farther and acknowledging the jurisdictional and *official* (not "infallible"!) doctrinal competence of a possible future institution of unity.

Thus, *first of all,* it was inevitably overlooked that a concrete institution of unity has neither function nor meaning if it cannot undertake initiatives that would effect and represent this unity in historical form, either in the minimal and compromising manner of the World Council of Churches, or in the excessively absolutist manner of the contemporary papacy. *Secondly,* in the name of the freedom of the Gospel, only an undifferentiated "no" could be spoken to the doctrinal claim of the papacy. But if it has been considered that official doctrinal statements on the part of an institution of unity are not immediately concerned with "truth," but only have an "official" character, then further discussion would have been possible. Such statements represent a reasonable compromise and an attempt not to offend or out-trump anyone, and they do not arise in an excessive and dictatorial fashion. Our Protestant brothers, too, acknowledge the meaningfulness of "official" confessional formulas.

However, if models for a future institution of unity are to be effective ecumenically, they cannot be developed on the basis of a monarchical governing office. In this respect, only the voluntary "renunciation of sovereignty" is conceivable, or—as the Protestant side proposed—solutions which *de facto* amount to a renewed renunciation of any historical expression of unity (recognition of a "primacy" devoid of jurisdiction). For only *corporate* models can be adequate to the complexities of present and future situations. Only such models provide concrete methods of achieving approximate unity without the use of force, and in this fashion guaranteeing defense against the tyranny of political majorities, and the protection of small groups.

For example, a "World Council of Churches" is conceivable,

with its "permanent chairman" being the bishop of Rome acting as *primus inter pares*. This institution of unity would only be competent in matters of "interconfessional" ecumenical interest, but it would have a minimal and basic official character for effective jurisdiction and the formulation of doctrine. The individual member churches would continue to exist in their concrete forms, with their own traditions of practice and theory and their diverse institutional structures. Nevertheless, such a World Council would still necessitate decisive changes for the individual Churches. Through their recognition of this overarching ecumenical institution, they would be de-confessionalized and obligated to a measure of concrete historical unity. On the other hand, such a "World Council" would have the right and the duty (hence the "jurisdiction"!) to prevent violations of the spirit of Christian community in all dimensions of Church life and to correct them by interventions, initiating discussions, etc. *This kind* of competence in jurisdiction and doctrine, while minimal and basic, and hence restricted to "ecumenical" matters, would be desirable and beneficial in order to avoid the further development of particularistic traditions that only lead to the formation of ghettos.

Perhaps these or similar concepts will never become reality. But there do not seem to be any real alternatives. Retention of the "Catholic *a priori*"—with whatever modifications—only serves to restrict the unity of churches to a so-called "spiritual" realm, causing Christianity to miss the opportunity to realize and make evident the power of the Gospel to create community.

Notes

Introduction

[1] Ignaz von Döllinger, *Das Papsttum* (unchanged reprint of the 1892 Munich edition=Janus, *Der Papst und das Concil*) (Darmstadt, 1969), pp. viii, ix.

[2] *Enchiridion symbolorum definitionum et declarationum de rebus fidei et morum*, edited by H. Denzinger, in the revised edition by A. Schönmetyer (Barcelona-Rome-Freiburg, 1967—abbreviated DS) nos. 3053-3064.

[3] DS, nos. 3065-3075.

[4] DS, no. 3055.

[5] Briefly summarized in the Canon, DS, no. 3058.

[6] *Idem.*, DS no. 3064.

[7] DS, no. 3074.

[8] Charles Davis, "Questions for the Papacy Today," in *Papal Ministry in the Church* (*The New Concilium*, Vol. 64), edited by Hans Küng (New York, 1971), p. 18. (Subsequently cited as *Papal Ministry*.)

[9] Janus, (n. 1), p. xiii.

Chapter One

[1] For the following study, see: Rudolf Pesch, "The Position and Significance of Peter in the Church of the New Testament," in *Papal Ministry*, pp. 21-35, 245; Felix Christ, "Das Petrusamt im Neuen Testament," in Denzler, Christ, Trilling, Stockmeier, de Vries, Lippert, *Zum Thema Petrusamt und Papsttum* (Stuttgart, 1970), pp. 36-50; Wolfgang Trilling, "Ist die katholische Primatslehre schriftgemäss?" *ibid.*, pp. 51-60.

[2] Christ, p. 37.

[3] Oscar Cullmann, *Petrus. Jünger-Apostel-Märtyrer* (Zürich-Stuttgart, 1960).

[4] Pesch, p. 27.

[5] Cf. Christ, pp. 39, 40.

[6] Josef Blank, "The Person and Office of Peter in the New Testament," in *Truth and Certainty* (*The New Concilium*, vol. 83), edited by E. Schillebeeckx and B. van Iersel (New York, 1973), p. 49.

[7] Pesch, pp. 27 f.

[8] Cf. Christ, p. 42.

[9] See below, Chap. 2.

10 Cf. Christ, p. 42.
11 *Ibid.*, p. 38.
12 *Ibid.*, p. 45.
13 Trilling, p. 56.
14 Gunter Bornkamm, "Die Binde-und Lösegewalt in der Kirche des Matthäus," in *Die Zeit Jesus (Festschrift fur H. Schlier)* (Freiburg, 1970), pp. 93-107.
15 Pesch, pp. 28-30.
16 In support of this late date, Bornkamm (*loc. cit.*, p. 104) refers to the fact that the resurrection of Jesus is already presupposed. The delay in the second coming of Christ is also presupposed, and the Church has to make its arrangements for the duration of secular time. The origin of the Christian community which called itself "Church" lies in the sphere of Hellenistic-Jewish Christianity. This self-designation contains a "theological program" directed against the Synagogue. "The meaning of the ekklesia ... is no longer confined to Israel, but is worldwide and purely Christological in its specification."
17 Blank, pp. 50-53.
18 Cf. Trilling, p. 54; Christ, p. 43.
19 Cf. Blank, *passim.*

Chapter Two

1 For the following, see Peter Stockmeier, "Das Petrusamt in der frühen Kirche," in Denzler, Christ, et al., pp. 61-79 and James McCue, "Roman Primacy in the First Three Centuries," in *Papal Ministry*, pp. 36-44.
2 Stockmeier, p. 63.
3 McCue, p. 38.
4 See below, Chap. 2-B, 1.
5 Blank, p. 54.
6 Stockmeier, p. 65.
7 *Adv. haer.*, III, 3, 1.
8 *Ibid.*, III, 3, 2. (Translation from K. Baus— see below, note 10, p. 356n.)
9 McCue, p. 40.
10 Karl Baus, *From the Apostolic Community to Constantine (Handbook of Church History*, edited by Hubert Jedin and John Dolan), (New York, 1965) I, 357.
11 *De praescr. haer.*, 32, 1.2.
12 *Ibid.*, 36, 1-3.
13 *History of the Church*, V, 23-24.
14 McCue, p. 40.
15 Cullmann, *passim.*
16 Cf. Eusebius, *History of the Church*, II, 15, 2.
17 Cullman, *passim.*

[18] I Clement 5, 3-5.

[19] Stockmeier, p. 64.

[20] *Ibid.*, p. 65.

[21] *Adv. haer.*, III, 1, 1.

[22] Cf. Eusebius, II, 25, 7.

[23] Baus, p. 117.

[24] *Ibid.*, p. 118. For more detailed information, see the entire section, pp. 115-118.

[25] *Ibid.*, p. 115.

[26] *Commentary on the Gospel of Matthew*, 12, 10.11.

[27] *Fifty-fourth Homily on Matthew.*

[28] *Explanation of the Psalms*, 40, 30.

[29] *Concerning the Mystery of the Incarnation of the Lord*, 4, 32.

[30] *Interpretation of the Gospel of John*, 7, 14.

[31] *De pudicitia*, 21, 9.

[32] Cf. B. Altaner and A. Stuiber, *Patrologie* (Freiburg-Basel-Wien, 1966), p. 159. "No satisfactory proof can be derived from *De pudicitia* that Tertullian was attacking a bishop residing outside of Africa.... Tertullian plainly directs his attack against Bishop Agrippinus of Carthage."

[33] Baus, p. 360.

[34] McCue, p. 42.

[35] Baus, p. 363.

[36] See below, Chap. 3-A, 4.

Chapter Three

[1] McCue, p. 43.

[2] *Ibid.*

[3] "Decretum Gelasianum," DS, nos. 350-351. (The antiquity of these texts is not uncontested either.)

[4] Cf. McCue, p. 44.

[5] Cf. Carl Mirbt and Kurt Aland, *Quellen zur Geschichte des Papsttum und des römischen Katholizismus*, Vol. 1: *Von den Anfängen bis zum Tridentum* (Tübingen, 1967), pp. 171-172.

[6] McCue, p. 44.

[7] Stockmeier, p. 76; cf. pp. 76-78 for the following. Further, Wilhelm de Vries, "Theoretical and Practical Renewals of the Primacy of Rome. The Development after Constantine," in *Papal Ministry*, pp. 45-49.

[8] Stockmeier, p. 76.

[9] "Response of Innocent I to a Letter of the Synod of Mileve": cf. Mirbt and Aland, I, 186.

[10] Letter 15, cf. Mirbt and Aland, I, 197, 198.

[11] Letter 14, 1, cf. Mirbt and Aland, I, 197.

[12] de Vries, p. 47.

[13] Stockmeier, p. 78.

14 Cf. Mirbt and Aland, I, 208.
15 Stockmeier, p. 79.
16 *Ibid.*, p. 78.
17 Cf. G. Schwaiger, *Papst*, in LThK VIII, 36, 37.

Chapter Four

1 de Vries, p. 48.
2 *Ibid.*, p. 48 f.
3 Johannes Haller, *Das Papsttum. Idee und Wirklichkeit*, Vol. I, *Die Grundlagen* (Reinbek, 1965), p. 221.
4 *Ibid.*, p. 217.
5 *Ibid.*, p. 222.
6 *Ibid.*, p. 277.
7 Eugen Ewig, "Die Abwendung des Papsttums vom Imperium und seine Hinwendung zu den Franken," in Jedin and Dolan eds., III, 1.
8 Haller, p. 292.
9 Cf. Ewig, [p. 17].
10 Haller, p. 298: "To sum it all up, then, there can be no doubt that, since the turn of the seventh to the eighth century, for the Franks as for the Anglo-Saxons, Peter, the prince of the Apostles and keeper of the gates of heaven, had become the most important saint.... He lives on in his earthly vicar, who therefore was owed service and obedience, which the saint... will repay in the next world."
11 E. Ewig, *Das Zeitalter Karls des Grossen* [*The Era of Charlemagne*], in Jedin and Dolan, eds., p. 94.
12 Horst Fuhrmann, "Theoretical and Practical Renewals of the Primacy of Rome from the Early Middle Ages until the Gregorian Reform," in *Papal Ministry*, p. 55.
13 Friedrich Kempf, *Kirchenverfassung, Kultus, Seelsorge und Frömmigkeit vom 8. Jh bis zur gregorianischen Reform* [*Church der, Cult, Pastoral Care and Piety* ...], in Jedin and Dolan, p. 319.
14 Cf. Fuhrmann, p. 55.
15 *Ibid.*, p. 56.
16 *Ibid.*, p. 57.
17 *Ibid.*

Chapter Five

1 Cf. Mirbt and Aland, I, p. 282.
2 Fuhrmann, p. 59.
3 F. Kempf, *Die gregorianische Reform* [*The Gregorian Reform*], in Jedin and Dolan, p. 429.
4 Fuhrmann, p. 58.
5 Cf. Mirbt and Aland, I, 460.

⁶ Cf. Karl August Fink, *Die Päpste in Avignon* (Kap. 37-40) [*The Popes in Avignon* (Chap. 37-40)], in Jedin and Dolan, p. 417.

⁷ This thesis agrees with the results of a meticulous historical study by Brian Tierney, *Origins of Papal Infallibility, 1150-1350. A Study on the Concepts of Infallibility, Sovereignty and Tradition in the Middle Ages* (Studies in the History of Christian Thought), edited by Heiko A. Oberman, Vol. 6 (Leiden, 1972). Cf. the review of this study by J. J. Hughes, in *Orientierung* 36 (1972), 183-185.

⁸ Tierney, p. 32.

⁹ *Ibid.*, p. 35.

¹⁰ Hughes, p. 184.

¹¹ Tierney, p. 159.

¹² Hughes, p. 184.

Chapter Six

¹ Joseph Lortz and Erwin Iserloh, *Kleine Reformationsgeschichte* (Freiburg, 1969), p. 19.

² *Ibid.*, p. 21.

³ Cf. *ibid.*, p. 14.

⁴ Cf. *ibid.*, p. 16.

⁵ H. Jedin, *Ursprung und Durchbruch* [*Origin and Breakthrough of the Catholic Reform to 1563*], in Jedin and Dolan, IV, 469.

⁶ H. Jedin, *Geschichte des Konzils von Trient*, Vol. II: *Die erste Trienter Tagungsperiode 1545-47* (Freiburg, 1957), pp. 308-309.

⁷ Jedin, *Origin and Breakthrough*, p. 519.

⁸ Joseph Lortz, *Geschichte der Kirche in ideengeschichtlicher Betrachtung. Eine geschichtliche Sinndeutung der christlichen Vergangenheit* (Münster, 1940), #70, IV, B 2 (III, 16).

⁹ Louis Cognet, *Das kirchliche Leben...* [*Church Life under the Influence of the Church State and the Enlightenment*], Chaps. 19-21, in Jedin and Dolan V, 410.

¹⁰ Otto von Corvin, *Der Pfaffenspiegel* (Munich, 1971), p. 111.

¹¹ Cf. E. Iserloh, *Der Kampf...* [*The Struggle for the Understanding of the Freedom of the Christian*], in Jedin and Dolan, IV, 208.

¹² Cognet, p. 411.

Chapter Seven

¹ Roger Aubert, *Die katholische Kirche...* [*The Catholic Church and the Revolution*], in Jedin and Dolan, VI, 68.

² von Döllinger, p. 244.

³ Karl Bihlmeyer and Hermann Tüchle, *Kirchengeschichte:* III: *Die Neuzeit und die neueste Zeit* (Paderborn, 1956), p. 309.
⁴ V. Conzemius, "Why Was the Primacy of the Pope Defined in 1870?" in *Papal Ministry,* p. 77.
⁵ *Ibid.*
⁶ von Döllinger, p. 238.
⁷ Cited in Conzemius, p. 78.
⁸ Cf. Conzemius, p. 79.
⁹ R. Aubert, *The Reorganization of the Churches,* Chaps. 3-6, in Jedin and Dolan, VI, 136.
¹⁰ *Ibid.*
¹¹ *Ibid.*
¹² Pouthas citation in Aubert, p. 128.
¹³ Rudolf Lill, *Historische Voraussetzungen des Dogmas vom Universalepiskopat und von der Unfehlbarkeit des Papstes,* in *Stimmen der Zeit,* 95 (1970), 297.
¹⁴ *Ibid.*
¹⁵ Cf. Lill, p. 297.
¹⁶ Cf. Lill, p. 298.
¹⁷ Cf. G. Söhngen, *Neuscholastik,* in LThK VII, 923.
¹⁸ von Döllinger, pp. 238, 239.
¹⁹ Cf. Lill, p. 298.
²⁰ *Ibid.,* p. 299.
²¹ *Ibid.*
²² Cf. Aubert, p. 151.
²³ Cf. Lill, p. 294.
²⁴ *Ibid.,* p. 300.
²⁵ Conzemius, p. 81.
²⁶ Lill, p. 300.
²⁷ Hans Küng, *Infallible? An Enquiry* (London, 1972), p. 74.
²⁸ *Ibid.,* p. 75; further, Lill, pp. 302, 303.
²⁹ Küng, p. 75.
³⁰ Conzemius, p. 80.
³¹ Küng, p. 75.
³² Conzemius, p. 79.
³³ Cf. Lill, p. 302.
³⁴ Cited in: H. Jedin, *Kleine Konziliengeschichte. Die zwanzig ökumenischen Konzilien im Rahmen der Kirchengeschichte* (Freiburg, 1961), p. 105. [*A Short History of the Councils.*]
³⁵ *Ibid.*
³⁶ *Ibid.,* p. 106.
³⁷ *Ibid.*
³⁸ *Ibid.,* p. 107.
³⁹ *Ibid.*
⁴⁰ *Ibid.*
⁴¹ Cf. above, Introduction, p. 6.
⁴² Jedin, p. 110.

43 Cited in Jedin, p. 111.
44 *Ibid.*, pp. 111, 112.
45 *Ibid.*, p. 112.
46 Cf. Jedin, p. 112.
47 Cited in Jedin, p. 116.
48 Cf. *Ibid.*, p. 117.
49 *Ibid.*, p. 118.
50 *Ibid.*, p. 170.
51 *Ibid.*, p. 123.
52 Küng, p. 104.
53 Lill, p. 303.
54 Cited in Conzemius, p. 75.

Chapter Eight

1 DS, no. 3070 (1836).
2 J. Ratzinger, *Primat*, in LThK VIII, 763.
3 *Ibid.*
4 *Ibid.*, p. 762.
5 *Ibid.*, p. 763.
6 *Ibid.*, p. 761.
7 *Schreiben der deutschen Bischöfe über das priesterliche Amt. Eine biblisch-dogmatische Handreichung*, No. 30 (Trier, 1969), pp. 48-59.
8 W. de Vries, *Die Kollegialität auf Synoden des ersten Jahrtausends*, in Denzler, Christ, p. 85.
9 *Ibid.*
10 *Ibid.*, p. 86.
11 *Ibid.*, p. 89.
12 On this point, see the recent argument between Hans Küng and Karl Rahner in *Stimmen der Zeit*, 186 (1970), 361-377 (Rahner), and 187 (1971), 43-64, 105-122 (Küng). Perhaps it has become clear that it is basically false to discuss "infallibility" in the context of the papacy. Whether "infallibility" is possible should be discussed in the context of *Gospel and Church*. The 1870 definition by contrast is concerned with the *legal* question, whether the Pope can speak for the whole Church.
13 Cf. A. Lang, *Unfehlbarkeit*, in LThK X, 483.

Chapter Nine

1 Ratzinger, p. 761.
2 *Ibid.*
3 Cf. Baus, p. 346.
4 A further principle, of course, is the fact that every ecclesiastical act, including the structure of the Church, must be in harmony with the Gospel. Thus, for example, every Church

authority must be directed to service, and not to domination.

[5] However, here, too, a negative fixation on conventional structures is often a very strong force, for example, the "anti-popism" of some churches. Thus, a traditional structure can still influence further development even if only in a negative manner.

[6] Karl Rahner, "Die Träger des Selbstvollzugs der Kirche," in *Handbuch der Pastoraltheologie*, I (Freiburg, 1970), 196.

[7] Cf. John Lynch, "Advantages and Drawbacks of a Center of Communication in the Church. 1. Historical Point of View," in *Papal Ministry*, pp. 95-100.

[8] Rahner, p. 212. However, Rahner justifies this principle of subsidiarity by the "divine right" of the episcopate. This is merely a feudalist correction of strict absolutism. In fact, in the long run, an office of unity cannot function without recognition of this principle, whether there are bishops at all or some other intermediate institutions.

Chapter Ten

[1] When using the concept "universal Church," one should always keep in mind that there exists no organization today which could represent it, at least until the Catholic Church joins the World Council of Churches. One often speaks in an ideological fashion about the "universal Church" in Catholic theology, when only the whole *Catholic* Church is meant.